Depressi

Be Fu

Helen McNallen

chipmunkapublishing
the mental health publisher
empowering people with depression

Published by
Chipmunkapublishing
PO Box 6872
Brentwood
Essex CM13 1ZT
United Kingdom

http://www.chipmunkapublishing.com

All illustrations by Michelle Barrett

Chipmunkapublishing gratefully acknowledge the support of Arts Council England.

FOREWORD

I have known Helen for many years ever since she had the idea of a website and book that would help other people with depression. I have been with Helen as her ideas have taken shape and developed and we have spent many evenings discussing her book and I am delighted to see it come to fruition. I am also delighted to see how Helen has gone from suffering with horrible depression to someone who is happy and living her life to the full.

I believe that everything happens for a reason and Helen has used her own suffering to help other people and give them hope that things will get better. Having worked with many depressed patients myself I often find that their greatest problem is that they believe they cannot be helped and will never get better and nothing will work for them, they believe their depression is insurmountable.

Helen's book proves that this is simply not true and that there are cures and lifelines for coping with and overcoming depression. Furthermore those who are depressed find it almost impossible to concentrate and take in information so Helen has taken this into account and the style of her book is easy to read, warm, funny and full of hope and optimism. She has written it in such an accessible way that you take in the information easily and remember it effortlessly. 'Depression Can Be Fun' offers so much more than a light at the end of the tunnel, it is a beacon of inspiration and I would recommend it to anyone who is depressed or a carer, parent or partner of someone who is depressed. Helen is such a caring understanding person who has been there and so her information is invaluable, she understands all the complex issues concerning depression.

'Depression Can Be Fun' shows the reader how to cope and how to recover from depression in a way that is unique as Helen's approach is so different she combines refreshing honesty with humour even about her bleakest moments. Her book is insightful, caring, entertaining and searingly honest and in harmony with current medical thinking that depression does not make you negative but being negative and critical about yourself can certainly make you depressed.

Even when the cause of depression is chemical imbalances in the brain, new studies show that changing negative behaviours can change brain chemistry. This book shows you how to do this along with a host of other advice including dietary, vitamins, lifestyle and many other new and proven techniques.

I would not hesitate to recommend this book to any of my patients as I am a big fan of what Helen is doing to help people which is why I am honoured to write this introduction for her and to work on her website as a counsellor/advisor.

If you are a person who is suffering from depression this book will give you the insight that many sufferers can never find when they need it.

Marisa Peer
psychotherapist /hypnotherapist /behavioural expert /author/ broadcaster/ lecturer/
therapist of the year

CONTENTS

ACKNOWLEDGEMENTS

Gosh, there are so many people I would like to thank.

First and foremost I would like to thank my husband[1], Duncan. Without his care, love, patience, loyalty and support, I would not be here today. He gave me all this despite my blaming him initially for part of my Depression. I hope he can forgive me for that.

Secondly I would like to thank my family for all their support and to apologise to them for all the worry I have caused them during my illness.

My poor father was dragged back home so many times from business trips and holidays over a period of five years for one crisis or another to do with my illness. Parents live through their children's pain with them; I feel terribly guilty for the anguish and heartache I have caused him. Hopefully he is now feeling my enlightenment too. Thankfully it seems he is. The last time I saw him, he looked like my dad again and not the tortured, troubled man I've witnessed over the last few years.

My sister, Liz, has always been the voice of reason. Surprisingly she's always been the 'Black Sheep' of the family but the metamorphosis into the most special, caring, strong (that's a nice word for stubborn!) sister anyone could ever wish for was worth the wait. She has been my rock.

[1] Helen and Duncan are separated but remain good friends.

My little brother, Brendan, (at 30 years old, 6'2" and built like an athlete, he is still my little brother) couldn't have gone further away from the family if he'd tried. I'm sure that wasn't intentional! He just happened to find the woman of his dreams in Japan while he was travelling the world – she is wonderful. He has always been my voice of reason even from thousands of miles away and I would like to thank him for that. It was his idea to set up the website chat room so that people can talk to each other and to have therapists online. Not only grounded but clever! Finally I have taken his advice and set up www.depressioncanbefun.com. I've listened to him, even though he won't believe me as his famous last words are that we never listen to him. Well Brendan, here it is the end result. I did listen!

My second family whom I hold so dear and would like to thank is my husband's family. My mother- and father-in-law have always been so kind and loving and helped me in so many ways. My husband and I moved up to Scotland so that I could stay with them when my husband was travelling on business. It's like my second home. My sisters-in-law are the best in the world. I love them dearly and they must love me to be as patient with me as they have been and still want to spend time with me. They were the only people I felt comfortable staying with when Duncan went away. There was no pressure to do anything other than be myself. I could just go to bed but know that there was someone there. Just like when I was at home with Duncan.

My friends too have always been there for me and I never underestimate the value of their friendship, particularly my girlfriends from my student days who must have felt like we were sharing a house again I spent so much time staying with them before my husband and I moved to Scotland. They are like family to me. I'm very lucky. Thank you girls.

Also I have to thank my doctors who have been so patient and understanding despite my totally out of character hysteria at times which caused me to be rude and aggressive. My thanks go to Dr Eric Shur at The Priory Hospital Roehamptom and Dr Nihara Krause for the early years of my Depression. My special thanks go to Dr Tim Rogers at Herdmanflat Hospital for his unswerving support ever since.

My wonderful hypnotherapist, Marisa Peer has been amazing. She's a very kind person with great skill, talent, understanding, knowledge and powers of healing. She is a world of calmness, yet great fun. She's now busy helping the rest of the world and travelling much of the time but we still manage to talk about our lives.

Also I want to thank my friend and psychic, Emile Riley, whom I hold in very high regard as a very special person. He really cares about people and has really helped me and given me hope when I was lost.

My personal trainer, Nigel McHollan, deserves a special thank you. He has not only helped me to shed the four stone that I gained so quickly in the early stages of my Depression but didn't have enough energy to do anything about for a long time; he has been an excellent listener too. He knows practically everything about me and thank goodness is the sole of discretion. I can strongly recommend him.

I have also had the great pleasure of meeting Lulu Guinness who inspires me. I have always adored her fashion like most of the female population (how could you not!). Through my shopping addiction I am the proud owner of several of her wonderfully quirky and elegantly designed handbags, make-up bags, shoes, perfume and spectacles and more recently, her girlie pink flip flops (circa 2006)! She became even more of an inspiration when I learned that she has achieved her dream despite a long battle with depression. She certainly should give everyone hope. On sharing experiences of our stays in The Priory in London, she smiled "I have never laughed as much as on my psychiatrist's couch". When I told her I was writing this book, she said that "passing on the word is important". I hope you agree and you will pass the word on too.

A lot of people have helped and been there for me through the good and the bad times of my Depression and I have met many wonderful people during my illness whom I would not have met if I had not been ill. I'm not sure what people thought when they met me though given my sometimes 'strange' behaviour and often 'over the top' acting skills to cover up the depression!

If I have forgotten anyone, I'm sorry; I blame it on my loss of memory due to my ECT (electro convulsive therapy). A terrible experience but it comes in very useful sometimes. Selective memory, my ex-husband calls it!

There are always people to thank who will never know their contribution but I would like to extend this thank you to everyone who has touched me in some way and helped me on my road to recovery.

Without the help, support, inspiration and patience of all these people I would not have written this book.

Thankfully my family, friends and I are now able to talk and laugh about many of the things that have happened during and as a cause of my illness and it was them and my psychiatrist who said I should write about it, even lecture on it.

I was amazed at how many people were interested in my journey. I was invited onto This Morning to talk to Eamonn Holmes and Ruth Langsford and LK Today to talk to Lorraine Kelly and lots of TV and radio interviews all over the world. I felt quite uncomfortable about that. I didn't want people to think that I think that I am so special and my life so special that I would want to write about it and expect other people to want to read about it. I have written about it though in the hope that it will help others in some way too. I hope that it makes you laugh and gives everyone hope, even if you don't need it, but let's face it, hope and laughter never did anyone any harm that I know of.

I am dedicating this book to my father who has always been a great inspiration to me. If I ever become in some small way such a role model to my children (I haven't got any yet but you know what I mean!), I would be very happy.

He has always taught us the importance of laughter and he has certainly practised what he preaches despite all the hardship that life has thrown at him. Thank you Dad!

I would also like to acknowledge and thank you for picking up this book and letting me talk to you.

Well done, you've picked up the book, you're on your way. I wish you peace and happiness and a normal life again (whatever that is!).

Helen

INTRO

Hello to you and a very warm welcome to my book, Depression Can be Fun. My therapist suggested I write this book after I set up a website of the same name (www.depressioncanbefun.com). Yes, I know what you are thinking: “Can it really?” Join me in my experience and read on and see.

I hope you’re well and that today’s been good to you so far.

I wonder what your reason is for picking up this book.

Maybe it’s out of curiosity, maybe you yourself are suffering or have suffered from depression, or maybe you know someone, a loved one or a dear friend or colleague who is or may be suffering from depression. I wish that it could be the first ‘Maybe’ for everyone and that none of you have had to go through or will ever go through the depression that cripples people’s lives. But let’s get real here, if the statistics are correct (and who am I to doubt them!) currently three million people in Britain alone are diagnosed with depression, which in varying degrees affects most people at some stage in their lives. Apparently only half of the people suffering from depression actually seek medical help. The other half go into comedy!

My name is Helen McNallen. I have officially suffered with depression since 1999. When I say officially, that is when I finally conceded to seeing a doctor about my condition and the doctor officially diagnosed my clinical depression in spring 1999. I had been doing some very strange things for up to a year before that however, which would have set alarm bells ringing if I had known then what I know now.

But if I look back now at how unhappy I was in my job, the stress I was under at work, the long hours that I was working versus the hours I was resting, and my obsession with organising my home life and keeping fit and worrying about everyone else, it was a potent recipe for depression.

Unhappiness in one area of your life often leads to unhappiness in most other areas of your life and it can be very easy to blame the wrong area of your life as the culprit for your unhappiness.

My job was my unhappiness but for a long time I blamed my husband. Both my job and my husband were NEW in my life and I felt like my Depression was NEW. I blamed the wrong one.

I now know that there is little point blaming others for our unhappiness because only we can ALLOW that unhappiness to happen to us or ALLOW someone or something to keep doing something to us that is making us unhappy. So we can make ourselves happy. We don't have to rely on others to make us happy either through a relationship or friendship or a job.

I was initially diagnosed with mental and physical exhaustion by my doctor but when the psychiatrists got their hands on me, I was more precisely diagnosed as suffering from 'Clinical Depression'. Despite three years of intensive treatment, therapy, hospitalisation and TLC from my husband and respective families, I remained suicidal. My diagnosis was eventually modified to 'Bipolar'.

Depression Can Be Fun

It was Churchill who described his Depression as his 'Black Dog'. I think that this analogy is very clever as it suggests both familiarity and mastery. Depression is a beast that needs to be fed to survive. It sinks its teeth into a person but it is after all, only a dog, and it can be trained, controlled and locked up! You can learn how to train and control it. You can learn what it thrives on and how to starve it by looking closely at your own needs.

Your life does not have to stop. It does not have to limit your life. Many people who suffer from depression learn how to control it and lead full and successful lives. Think about what the following people have achieved while struggling with depression: Alexander the Great, General Paton and Napoleon, artists and writers such as Geothe and Tols. Some of the funniest people on the outside have had or are suffering from depression. Just look at Stephen Fry, Robin Williams, Jim Carrey, Jack Dee, Roseanne Barr, Spike Milligan, and Ruby Wax.

I have met many successful business men and women who are suffering from depression. It is a shame that they are not able to enjoy their lives and their success. Being depressed does not have to stop you achieving anything in your life. How great would it be to be able to enjoy your achievements, your success, and your life?

Anyone can suffer from depression until they learn to redirect it. Many people don't 'live' their lives today. They just exist. It makes them unhappy.

Depression seems to be an increasing phenomenon of the affluent 21st Century in which we find ourselves due to all the modern pressures of everyday lives. Working longer hours, low financial security, world recession and long term unemployment are just some of the modern pressures that lead many of us to depression.

Depression has now replaced back pain as the number one reason for taking time off work. So much so, that it is referred to as the common cold of mental illness and is the form of mental illness most frequently seen by psychiatrists, psychologists and physicians. The figures show that one in three people will experience depression at some time in their lives today.

Twenty years ago depression in children was almost unknown. Now the fastest increase in depression is amongst young people[2]. Another frightening report by the World Health Organisation estimates that by the year 2020, depression will be the second biggest cause of death and disability in the world.

Statistics also say that each year about one person in every thousand in Britain is treated in hospital for depression, 15 in every thousand consult their doctors about feeling depressed while even more do not seek medical advice and try to cope with the illness alone. This is a big problem.

---

[2] In a recent study by the Queen Elizabeth Medical Centre in W Australia, of 400 children aged 9-12, 16 were found to be clinically depressed, with 112 assessed as being vulnerable to future depression. The depressed children believed that happiness is achieved through the acquisition of fame, money and beauty. The happier children tended to believe that feeling good comes from healthy attitudes and pursuing worthwhile goals.

Depression Can Be Fun

According to the Mental Health Foundation, depression is the cause of 50-75 per cent of all suicides in Britain each year.

If you are suffering from depression, you should be patting yourself on the back for even picking up this or any book. I really mean that. I didn't read anything apart from glossy magazines for the first four years of my Depression and even then all I did was look at the pictures. That's why you'll find pictures in this book!

You might not feel able or want to read or concentrate on anything right now or feel that you still can't – 'still', a word that apparently I used to use a lot during the worst stages of my Depression. "I still can't do this!!"

I basically sealed my own fate for the next seven years with the meaning and emotion that I gave to my situation. I convinced myself that NO THING (NOTHING) mattered in my life. It makes sense that the emotion you live with dictates the quality of your life. With such negative emotion, how could I be anything other than depressed?

I cannot make everyone happy (I wish I could) but I hope that you can smile and maybe even giggle as you read this book and my experiences that I can now laugh at (well most of them anyway – some of them I'm still god damn embarrassed about!). The fact that I have written this book and that I can laugh now makes me realise that I am getting better. Laughter is so important. I've missed it.

Right now you are feeling like this is the worst thing that has ever happened to you but it could be the best. Just remember "It's always the darkest just before the dawn".

Depression Can be Fun.

Read on and see.

IT'S GOING TO BE FINE

"Change your lifestyle, it will end in tears!"

So, you know what, it's fine. Anything you can do right now is fine! Please believe me. Depression is bad enough to deal with without putting additional pressure on yourself. That does not give you permission to stop trying. It just gives you permission not to be too hard on yourself while you are trying. Frustration is good as it encourages us to keep trying. Feeling like there is no solution is depression.

The problem with depression is that it does not make you feel like trying. Your negative focus and feelings make you not feel like trying anything. That negative momentum is paralysing.

The human mind can trick us to believe that everything is negative. All day we ask and answer our own questions. Thinking is nothing but a process of asking and answering questions of our subconscious or conscious[3]. With depression we constantly question.

"WHY DOES IT ALWAYS HAPPEN TO ME?" Negative questions generate negative answers. Ask a lousy question, get a lousy answer.

Whatever you focus on feels real to you. When we attach words to it, it gives it meaning. It becomes our experience. Who do we talk to most? – Ourselves. Need I say more! Depressed people often doubt themselves and their abilities in all kinds of ways, but seldom in their judgment about their own interpretation of things! Be conscious of words that create your emotions. If you say certain phrases often enough, you believe them. You can always find a way to back up what you believe.

When you are depressed, you believe that you are not in control of events in your life. It is this sense of control that is so important. We often find ourselves in situations where we have little control – such as waiting for the result of a medical examination, waiting to learn whether someone still wants to be our lover, or waiting for exam results. What can we do apart from eat chocolate, light up a cigarette or bite our nails?

3

Apparently the average human being has 65 000 unique thoughts in a day. The only problem is that 95% of those thoughts are the same ones as yesterday.

The only control we have during these times is internal. By exercising control over how and when we act or react, we can retain a sense of control. When I took my A levels (as they were called in the good old days) I felt sure that I had not done well but I knew that I would have to wait all summer to find out exactly how badly I had done. I visualised getting bad results and reacting calmly and planned that I would re-sit in a beautiful college that I had always wanted to study in. So that's what I did. My two best friends didn't get the results they needed for university either so we all went to the beautiful college together!

Some advice for which I had to pay a lot of money and didn't listen to at the time, but you might find helpful now is:

Take a limited number of days in which you will not dwell upon nor mention your Depression or the cause of your Depression (if you know it) for more than the briefest moment (just enough so as not to be rude).
Put aside a period in which to problem solve of one or two hours per day, rather than worry around and about whenever thoughts come into your head.
Become a mistress/master of your own emotions, rather than be at the beck and call of the circumstances and other people.

I liked the sound of that and it all makes sense. I wish it had made sense at the time and that I could have acted on it sooner but I obviously wasn't ready. It is all good advice. I can see that now. Maybe it will help you one day too. You can always make a note of it. One more note on one more piece of paper to add to your clutter, I know!

I was wrapped up with all my negative and distorted and exaggerated thoughts. They were confused and racing. A double whammy! All I did was think but I still wasn't getting anywhere because I was thinking negatively emotionally and not objectively. The mire would just become darker, thicker and more hopeless. The sense of doom and gloom was overpowering.

If I could have spent as much time thinking positive thoughts about how to deal with my situation instead of negative, I would have conquered Everest. The power of thought is incredible, both positive and negative. I really do believe now that you become what you think and negativity attracts negativity. It's also been proven clinically that the way we think actually changes our cellular chemistry.

The positive emotions OPTIMISM, HOPE, FAITH, LOVE and HAPPINESS (just in case you've forgotten what they are! I know I did) are totally linked to a strong immune system. Negative emotions and feelings (which I won't write in capital letters as we don't need those reinforcing): helplessness, anger, depression, pessimism, hopelessness and sadness weaken the immune system in the body, making you more susceptible to illness.

As I said, I believe that negativity attracts negativity. If you need proof of this, just think about how your day goes if you wake up thinking that it will be a bad day. It normally is and you are proved right. Why do you think that is? You're not a fortune teller. If you were, you'd be doing it for a living. You will notice that bad things happen and again, in many subtle ways, you will make bad things happen. If you think it will be a good day, it will be. You will notice the good things and again, in many subtle ways, you will make good things happen.

I'm not naively saying that if we all think positively every day, we'll all have good days every day. We cannot change much of our circumstance but we can decide what attitude to take towards it and that attitude affects the quality of our life.

We all know that this is easier said than done. We all have the tools to do it ourselves and just need to be shown how to use them. By now all of us have developed some ways of thinking based on our past experiences that may not be helpful to us but are dictating and responsible for our behaviour and emotions. If we get to the underlying problem, we can challenge our negative thoughts and emotions and replace them with positive, more rational and realistic behaviour and thoughts that are more appropriate and helpful.

Do not worry if you have a long list of problems or if you have a particular problem that you have had for many years. From my experience, just because you have more than one problem or have had a problem for many years, it doesn't necessarily mean that any therapy or solution will be harder or longer.

We do not all have the know-how to deal with our own problems systematically and thoroughly. We haven't all spent years studying psychology and even if we had, we may well not be able to put it into practice on ourselves. Some of the best psychologists in the world have therapy themselves. It has always been easier to spot and resolve someone else's problems when you are not emotionally involved. So no one should feel weak or embarrassed about seeking professional help.

You often find that your own mind runs round in circles hour after hour, day after day and you are not able to escape the rut you are in. Maybe talking to your family, friends, colleagues or whomever is involved in your life would help or to your doctor or a counsellor or psychiatrist or psychologist.

After all, if you have a problem with your accounts, you have no qualms about going to your accountant (other than the expense) and if you have a problem with your plumbing, you go to your plumber. You wouldn't dream of doing it yourself. Well my sister would but I wouldn't and if I did, I certainly would expect the job to be done much better by an expert. You wouldn't go to the plumber to sort out your accounts and vice versa. In class you put your hand up and ask a question of the teacher who will know the answer. Therefore if you are depressed, you should not feel awkward or uncomfortable about going to see someone who can help you. Do not be afraid to ask for help.

Help and advice can come in many forms from many sources which I will discuss later. You'll hear lots of advice from doctors, other sufferers, friends and family. Some will be good; some will be bad. But it could be good advice at the wrong time. Your mind and body might not be ready for advice. It might just need time right now to heal itself.

The American actress, Jennifer Aniston allegedly describes that need perfectly when questioned about how she was coping with her difficult relationships with her mother and her ex-husband, Brad Pitt. She said,

"I've read many self-help books. I believe in being an 'everythingist'. But right now I couldn't look at a self-help book if I was dying in the street and it told me how I didn't have to die in the middle of the street. I couldn't do it. I'm not in that place right now." That is what she felt was right for her at that time.

I'm not a doctor but I believe that my Depression was my body's way of self-preservation. It shut down so I couldn't carry on hurting it. It was my body's way of subconsciously helping. I would have just carried on fighting as I had been trying to do for two years when I felt that my life had no meaning. My mind wouldn't let me stop. I wouldn't stop. My husband could see the deterioration in my physical and mental state but could not persuade me to stop. My dad could not convince me to stop. I remember a long walk that my father and I took up the Fulham Road together. My dad was trying to convince me to stop and get help but I wasn't listening. I was like an obsessed robot, determined to work my way through it. "I'm fine. I will be fine. It will be fine". But I didn't feel fine and it wasn't fine and it wasn't going to be fine.

In the end, severe depression forces you then to give up that job, that relationship etc that has caused the depression because you are physically unable to carry on. Often that friend or partner who wasn't good for you leaves you anyway as they can't cope or don't want to cope or you drive them away. It's not you who makes the choice now. It's made for you and suddenly everything stops. That choice is taken out of your hands by your brain and your body.

Then you find yourself sucked into the black hole that you have been fighting against. You've fallen off your world into the abyss. Your world stops. You have left familiar territory which as terrible as it was, at least you knew what you were up against. The struggle begins. Right now though, you don't even want to get back to familiar territory. You don't care if you never get back there. You can't imagine getting back there. You can't get back there. All that energy and physical nervous energy that had been driving you on and pushing you forward suddenly vanishes and you become an empty vessel. The shock in itself is totally traumatic. You just do not know what to do. You cannot do anything. You find yourself paralysed with shock, fear and exhaustion.

For a while, or a long time in my case and a lot of cases, you feel like the world just passes you by and you get left behind. You just exist. You get up just to go back to bed. Nothing in between.

Eventually though, time 'does its thing' as it usually does and when that light starts to flicker again in your head, you will know and be ready to join the land of the living again.

This is very hard to believe when you are in the depths of depression. You think that anyone talking about the light at the end of the tunnel does not understand and does not know what they are talking about. I felt that too, really I did. I felt that for years. 'No one could possibly understand my pain, and what I was going through. No one understood that there was no light'.

If you can start to think positively, you can use this time to reassess yourself and your life. Positive thinking is productive thinking. This may be something that you choose to do yourself or it may work better for you to contact a therapist and work through it with them.

Others can often see something that we are totally blind to ourselves. A good therapist will know what the right questions are to ask you, so that you make the realisation yourself – far more empowering in my opinion.

Whatever it takes, the future is yours to choose and design physically and emotionally. We all have the choice and freedom to choose to be happy or sad. I know which one I'm aiming for.

This may seem like a mammoth task and a lot of changes to make and may take time. Depression is a major health problem. It threatens the very basis of your life. It stops you doing what you need to do, not only to survive, but to have fun and to achieve your goals. It may actually threaten your life if like me you become suicidal.

It's particularly vicious as it is compounded by the torment of the families and friends of those who are afflicted with the illness.

LOOK AFTER YOUR BRAIN. It is your home for this lifetime and if it falls apart on you then you will not be able to do all those things that you want to and deserve to do and enjoy. Don't degrade your life with empty aspirations. Life is meant to be respected, enjoyed and celebrated. You only get the one.

The vital point is that understanding, controlling and beating depression requires a set of skills and as such can be learned.

I am learning and putting into practice what I have heard others preach and practise themselves. You will find that I will repeat myself in this book. I've done this on purpose as I have found repetition important in my recovery and learning. Repetition is necessary. Often I didn't want to listen or it didn't go in the first time but by the second or third time I was listening and it was beginning to sink in!

Repetition is necessary because it is so easy to forget the advice and instructions that you don't want to hear. It is also easy to underestimate the importance of each step along the way. My husband used to be exasperated when I used to come out of an hour-long session with my cognitive therapist every week with a list of positive things to do and think to replace my negative ways and thinking and just slip back into my old routine of bad habits before the day was over. I just did what was the easiest for me at the time which was to slip back into my bad habits. Bad habits take a long time to become bad habits. It therefore takes time, determination and the right techniques to replace bad habits with good habits. You just need to keep reinforcing the positive: by doing the positive and thinking the positive and acting the positive, your mind will catch up and it becomes automatic.

Act the way you want to be and your mind will follow your behaviour. Depressives are great actors. We act so well in fact that often people do not see the turmoil going on beneath. We all deserve to be on that red carpet for our acting skills to cover up our Depression, so use it to your advantage to help trick your mind into incongruent behaviour. Soon your body and your mind end up believing it! Honestly, it really works. It has been proven to work. It's worked for me. Many of my friends say that I never seem to be unhappy and handle things so well. If only they knew what has been going on inside.

You cannot change what life throws at you but you can change how you react to it. I think I heard this somewhere before but how true it is that 'Life is something that happens when you have got something else planned'.

I try to believe and sometimes it helps me (sometimes it just pisses me off) to believe that things do happen for a reason. Not a good move to tell someone this at the wrong time of course! You may find yourself showered with a torrent of verbal abuse, or worse, depending on your timing!

A friend sent a text message to me after a tough few months with her husband being very ill and a toddler who was just finding her feet. It said, "Life's a Bitch for a reason. Sometimes it just takes her a lifetime to tell you why!" I bet we can all relate to that.

My aim in writing this book is in no way to make light of depression. Having experienced its debilitation and disorientated emptiness for almost 10 years I would never belittle what depression does to us and our loved ones.

I just want to try to help others capture that glimmer of hope that I lost sight of for a long time. I am writing what I felt like reading at the time when I was depressed. I think that we have forgotten how to be happy in our busy lives. We lose sight of what really matters and of family values that have always been so important in the past. Many of us need to learn how to be happy again. We deserve to be happy.

Maybe the information overload is to blame. Now that we have the internet and excessive media to show us how we should be living our lives and how the other half live, we feel forced to compare ourselves to other people.

I am sure that our grandparents had their own problems but speaking to many old people, they admit that the world was a much happier place when we had a lot less.

My friend's grandfather said to me "Those were the days and these are the times. We were poor but grateful. We helped one another. We were happy with what we had. We were content. Today people only help one another expecting something back. 'Self' and Greed have taken over from helping others and sharing. We are guilty of our own fate. Modern society promotes a mentality of always wanting more and of 'Grabbing' even when it is at the expense of others and our environment and brings a whole new meaning to the word 'survival'". That made me think. It also made me sad.

There still are a lot of nice people in this world (ooh, I do hate the word nice but that is exactly what I mean). And it is often the nice people who get depressed. I define 'nice people' as people who get on with things not making too much fuss, helping others, trying to be nice. Everyone tells me I'm a nice person! These people tend to get overlooked, taken for granted and taken advantage of precisely because they don't make a fuss and are easy to overlook. They often take too much on and don't shout for help when they are the ones who actually need it most. Yeah, I guess I am nice!

I am not advocating not being nice of course. Maybe I am advocating not being too nice for self-preservation and your sanity.

It is nice to be nice for good karma and to make the world a nicer place and see others happy is very rewarding. Maybe you believe 'what goes around comes around'. Maybe you believe that to be happy, you need to make others happy. Maybe you believe that before you receive, you need to give. We all mold, add, make up, and learn our own beliefs but I think that it is pretty much everyone's aim to be happy or if it isn't, it should be!

How often have you heard yourself and others say, 'All I want is to be happy, be in a loving relationship, and have a good job…' and then everything will be fine.

These are very good ultimate goals but they are too broad and not an easy request to make of your poor doctor or psychologist who unfortunately doesn't own a magic wand. If you can find out what is missing that will make you fine, that's a start. A famous psychologist uses this successful method with his patients to find out what would make them fine. He asks them to describe their perfect day. Think about it.

An unsuccessful author had never managed to finish a book. When he described his perfect day, it would be to wake up on his own island, have breakfast with the Spice Girls, jet across in his speed boat to a private beach and dance the afternoon away with Catherine Zeta Jones. There was no mention of his writing in his day. His patient wanted to be rich and famous and thought that he could achieve this through his writing. His patient saw writing as a means to becoming rich and famous and not as something he wanted to do or be. It was making him unhappy.

I have tried this on a couple of my friends (not myself yet!) and they found it really interesting.

I hope everyone appreciates that they deserve to be happy not only because being miserable and depressed is a terrible place to be but if as we are told, negativity is dangerous to our health, physically and emotionally, surely we all owe it to ourselves to work towards happiness.
My grandma always used to say "Without some lows, you cannot fully appreciate the highs'. It would be nice to be given the chance though wouldn't it? Why are grandmas always so sensible? I guess they've been around long enough to know.

It can be a comfort to know that many people share the same problems as you and that many get better. You are by no means alone, despite how isolated or unusual your mood makes you feel - depression is treatable. My psychiatrist's words still ring in my ears that:

'Depression is an illness and as such it can be treated and you will get better'.

However it is often of little comfort to a sick person to learn that he or she is not as sick as someone else. In fact it can often make us feel worse as it reduces the size of our thinking. My husband was prone to telling me when I had had a bad day that three people die every minute of AIDS in Africa and that I should think myself lucky. Yes it is terrible and I do want to help people living in poverty when I am feeling a little better but it's not what I need to hear when I'm in the depths of depression and sobbing into my pillow in despair. I know he was only trying to help but a cup of tea would be of far more help at such a time. Why do men always feel the need to find a solution to your problem, when there really isn't one?

I was depressed constantly for four years. I used to sleep for days and still wake exhausted. I could not get out of bed. When I was up, everything was an effort. I put on weight because I wasn't doing anything except eat and take my medication. My husband has since described me as a 'maggot'. Charming! He is right though. There was no mystery to the weight gain. I would move on from doughnuts to chocolate muffins to smoked cheese and crackers to cheese flavoured crisps. I wasn't eating because I was hungry or even because I wanted to. I was eating to try to fill a void. I hated myself. I didn't think that I was worth looking after. I abused myself physically, hitting and punching myself. I ate vast quantities of junk food that I would never have dreamed of eating when I was 'well'.

My mood swings were scary. The diet certainly wasn't helping. My body was infested with E numbers and chemicals that it had never been exposed to before. That combined with the depression was a recipe for disaster.

I remember throwing my mobile phone at my car windscreen one day while I was in the car with my husband and smashing the windscreen. We were in London in a Marks and Spencer car park. We couldn't go anywhere until we got it replaced. It was some throw! I can think of worse places to be stranded though. At least I didn't go hungry!

I remember throwing uncontrollable fits and tantrums in public and private. My husband must have felt like he was living with a time bomb. I remember my husband physically holding me down and trying to give me sedatives to calm me down.

It was the sheer frustration and desperation that led to my angry outbursts. I just did not know what to do with all the anger. I used to cry and shake uncontrollably and hide in my bed just sleeping or thinking about how dreadful and hopeless everything was. Apparently I would always be in the same foetal position, rocking and shaking with fear, despair and hopelessness. If it wasn't coming out as tears, it came out with outbursts of kicking and screaming. The endless sobbing was bad enough for my husband to listen to and deal with but at least that was harmless. How he coped with the physical blow outs, I will never know. How he coped with any of it, I will never know.

I think that I am the lucky one as I don't remember many of the dreadful episodes due to mental gaps in my memory after my ECT treatment that I will explain later. It was my poor husband, family and friends around me who had to live through all of it. Only now that I am better able to handle it, have they started to tell me the truth of what it was like. I just remember how terrible I felt all the time.

Gradually the variations in mood and extreme mood swings became less extreme and more stable and the good days would be more consistent. I would stay out of my bed a little longer and have a little more energy.

Now I am OK most of the time. When I do feel down, it is generally for no more than two days and I bounce back again. I am sure that as I continue to learn how to avoid the obvious pitfalls and manage my life more sensibly, do things that I enjoy more often and practise feeling good more than feeling bad so that it becomes habit, my Depression will be a thing of the past. That is my goal. We all need goals and dreams. They keep us excited, enthusiastic, motivated and focused. They keep us 'alive'.

My dad's dream is to own a Bentley Continental. He knows that he will probably never get one but it is a wonderful dream to keep him focused and enthusiastic. It's also become my dream. I'd like to buy him one. So he'll probably end up with two! Without focus, we are lost. That is what I lost. Enjoy making your own dream and enjoy the journey towards it! Everything is a dream before it becomes reality. Every business, every building, every school started as a dream. Dreams are the raw material of reality.

Like I said it will be fine. Fate or destiny too needs to be coaxed, sweet-talked and persuaded to assist you. Luck likes people who feel lucky. Heaven helps those who help themselves. If there is something you badly want, assume that you are perfectly entitled to attain this and start inviting it into your life. This includes getting better and being happy and anything else wonderful you would like to have in your life.

THE HAPPY PILLS

When I refer to the Happy Pills I am talking about antidepressants and tranquillisers. After all, that's what they are meant to do isn't it? Make us happy.

Like many things in life antidepressants don't always do what they say they do or what we expect them to do. We expect so much of antidepressants. No tablet can make us happy. I don't know anyone who feels 'great' on antidepressants (and I know a lot of people on them!). They don't make your problems go away or make you feel that they have gone away. They do not make you feel happy and nor do they guarantee that you won't feel depressed. They are much more subtle. They may lessen and help some of the symptoms. For example, you might have a bit more energy, be able to sleep a little better, think less unhappy thoughts, feel less anxious and be able to concentrate better which can make you therefore more responsive to some talking therapy, but antidepressants taken on their own without any accompanying therapy to understand, control and overcome depression will not make you happy.

Depression pulls you into a downward spiral of negative thoughts and emotions that can be so intense that the body displays physical symptoms. Antidepressants are designed to treat these symptoms and can be very effective in treating them, which explains why you might think that they are temporarily making you happy and why it is common to mistake the symptoms for the cause of depression.

The medical definition of an antidepressant is: a medication designed to treat or alleviate the symptoms of clinical depression.

Even the medical definition tells us that antidepressants treat the SYMPTOMS of depression. They do not treat the CAUSE of the depression.

It is not even known for certain how antidepressants treat the symptoms of depression and how they work to make us 'happy'. The most recent antidepressants are thought to work by slowing down the absorption of the feel-good proteins/happy hormones in the brain by nerve cells in the brain. Serotonin, noradrenaline (norepinephrine) and dopamine are thought to be the chemicals most involved in depression. Serotonin and noradrenaline are the neurotransmitter chemicals that makes us feel happy. Dopamine makes us feel motivated.

Antidepressants treat the 'chemical imbalance' of 'happy hormones' in the brain but the low levels associated with depression are not the cause of the condition. They are caused by excessive stress being placed on the mind. While boosting levels can be a very welcome temporary relief when we are feeling so down, when the medication is stopped most people find themselves back at square one again. So whilst antidepressant medication can be useful for some people in lifting severe depression symptoms quickly, it should not be the sole treatment for depression.

Medication combined with the right therapy and skills training can help you overcome depression. It's harder work than just pill popping but as with most things, the more you put in the more you get out. Medical treatment alone rarely works.

'The key is that you want long term change to take place', says Dr Dozois, PhD, director of science of the Canadian Psychological Association and a professor at the University of Western Ontario. 'Drugs don't do as much in the long run as teaching patients to change the way they think.' He says even a few sessions of cognitive therapy following successful antidepressant treatment can help reduce relapse[4].

The danger of high expectations of the antidepressants can often mean people stop trying for themselves. I saw many people in hospital do nothing else but take their medication day after day, week after week, month after month and year after year (I am not exaggerating when I say this. Some people take antidepressants for years on end) and wait for them to produce miracles. I did it myself for a long time because I was told to, not because it made me feel any better. Medication dominated my life. It accompanied every mealtime both at home and when I was in the hospitals. The queue at the medication trolley in the hospital still fills me with sadness. We all awaited our medication like Pavlov's dogs in anticipation of their dessert (if dogs get dessert!). We all awaited our dessert - which is what the med trolley became known as because it came round after every mealtime. Except that what you expect from a dessert and what you get from the

---

[4] On average 50% of people on antidepressants alone will relapse within one year. Several studies of cognitive therapy, which focuses on correcting negative thinking patterns, have shown that it's just as effective as medication for treating depression, and the risk of relapse is under 25%.

medication do not compare. Antidepressants themselves never live up to expectation.

Medication is neither a total solution nor a magical cure. For a start, it can be trial and error to find the antidepressant or combination of antidepressants that works for you. Different people react and respond differently to different drugs. Sometimes an antidepressant that worked very well for a friend of yours will not work for you. You may have to try more than one antidepressant to find one that works for you. But don't worry there are almost thirty different kinds of antidepressants on the market so your doctor has a good chance of finding one that suits you.

Also, patients often do not feel any better for several weeks. Although the drugs begin to do their job immediately it is very normal for the antidepressants to take between four to six weeks before you feel any better. This should not stop you from taking the drug regularly as instructed by your doctor. However if you do not feel that there is any change in your mood after six to eight weeks, you should go back to your doctor who can switch you to a different antidepressant. Sometimes a combination of two or more antidepressants is prescribed to achieve a better result. I was always very jealous of people who started to feel better almost as soon as they started taking their antidepressants and would moan to my husband asking why antidepressants worked so quickly for some people and never seemed to work for me.

Certain antidepressants can initially make depression worse, can cause anxiety, or make a patient aggressive, uneasy or acutely suicidal which I always thought wasn't a great advert for antidepressants. As if our Depression isn't bad enough when we go to the doctors for help, the help that they offer could make us feel worse before we feel better!

I was always confused by my doctor talking about different kinds of antidepressants such as SSRIs, SNRIs and tricyclics and MAOIs. I've never trusted abbreviations that I don't understand so I did my research.

Basically there are four main groups of antidepressants. SSRIs (selective serotonin reuptake inhibitors) and SNRIs (selective serotonin/norepinephrine reuptake inhibitors) antidepressants are the most recent and have less side-effects and are less serious if taken in overdose than the original MAOIs (monoamine oxidase inhibitors) and tricyclic antidepressants.

Since the 1950s pills have dominated the treatment of depression. I am grateful that I was lucky enough to be prescribed therapy and medication as I feel I got more out of the therapy than the medication.

The pill box and pill popping practically dominate your day when you are ill. Every day was the same.

If I wasn't not popping those pills three times a day after meals, it was at least twice a day; often with that essential morning 'snack' of Valium (diazepam) at 11 am to 'take the edge off things' and make the rest of the day bearable; or the 5 o'clock Valium which replaces afternoon tea and has become necessary because I did not take the 11 o'clock one in an effort not to become totally dependent.

If I hadn't taken Valium, I would probably have used alcohol or smoking (if my mother hadn't given me a cigarette at the age of nine and the memory of almost throwing up and choking on it hadn't managed to put me off for life) or sex (a common side-effect of depression is loss of libido so right then that wasn't an option!); anything I could, just to give me respite from the pain in my head. I just could not bear it any longer. By 5 o'clock, the day really has become unbearable. You wish in the worst way that you had taken a Valium at 11 o'clock and avoided a whole day of anguish.

Everyone finds something that they think makes them feel better, whether it be drugs, drinking, smoking, sex or food. These things don't really make you happy and when the effect wears off, you need to do it again.

Afterwards I would just want to go to sleep as, when I was asleep, I could escape the pain for a few hours. I hoped that I would die in my sleep so I didn't have to wake up and feel that awful sense of despair, loss and helplessness. I felt like a complete burden to everyone and a complete waste of space.

I used to reprimand myself that if I'd taken my Valium when I needed it, I might have been feeling OK and been able to stay up and watch my soaps (the highlight of my day!) and go to bed at 8.30 pm when they'd finished. At least that was an almost respectable time to go to bed. 5.30 pm bedtime is definitely depressed man's time zone.

I still felt depressed on the antidepressants, but off the wall at the same time, sleepy and numb. Four horrible feelings rolled into one really. Four years in bed sleeping and only waking up to stuff my face or watch

TV, which were my only respite in life – in particular jam doughnuts of which I could happily down several a day in front of 'Richard and Judy' and 'This Morning'.

I didn't know what soaps and chat shows were before my Depression and have to say I preferred it when I didn't, because I have come to associate them with my Depression and they are depressing enough as it is without being depressed before they start! I used to try so hard to make it past that 5 o'clock barrier because if I didn't, that was another night that I would write off and leave my husband on his own again downstairs watching the TV. Even he used to be aware of the 'witching hour'. He would judge my mood by what time I used to go to bed. I didn't even think about cooking him dinner before I went. I didn't consider him at all actually. I suppose he could have left me. I suppose he should have left me. I couldn't have blamed him. I didn't even consider that scenario and if he had, it was no less than I deserved as far as I was concerned.

Maybe I just presumed he wouldn't. Maybe I didn't care. Maybe I would have felt even worse if that were possible. Although apart from feeling depressed, I don't think I had any real feelings about much while I was taking my meds (medication). In fact I just felt pretty numb.

Here's my preferred version of my pill box. I've replaced the am/pm boxes with activities that made me feel better.

My New Pill Regime

Monday	Tuesday	Wednesday	Thursday	Friday	Saturday	Sunday
Look forward to waking up as you're going to make yourself a cup of tea or coffee and go back to bed, watch TV or read the paper for half an hour.	Make yourself a healthy fruit or veggie smoothie.	Act as if you're the way you want to be. You might be surprised; your mind will want to follow.	Have a manicure-a real feel good treat! Something you can see 24/7, your new brightly coloured talons-no black!	Burn an uplifting aromatherapy candle. Throw all the windows open whilst doing the chores.	Meditate. You don't need training. Just positive visual imagery! A great positive invigorating way to start the day.	**LIE IN!**
Go for a walk with a dog or a friend for company. You don't have to buy a dog, borrow one; the owner will welcome the break!	Do a Yoga class or video, even if it's just to do the meditation at the end. You'll soon be addicted!	Do something nice for someone that makes you feel good about yourself.	Try a Pilate's class. Classes for all levels of skill, energy, and ages, great results! I promise you!	Wear your favourite perfume that reminds you of happy times/people.	Buy a new CD of a new artist you are not familiar with.	Go out to lunch.
Buy and send a funny card to a friend.	Listen to happy songs and resist the temptation to play music that reflects your mood.	Go out for a coffee, maybe with a friend. A book makes being on your own very acceptable. There are loads of cafés and bookshops. No excuses!	Read a gossip/trashy magazine.	Go for a massage/Indian head massage.	Write down a list of activities that give you pleasure, and do 1 a month.	Read the Sunday papers, (these are usually out of bounds as most news is depressing). Sunday is different BE A REBEL!
Reward yourself with a high cocoa content chocolate, don't feel guilty, it's for medicinal purposes, for boosting those serotonin levels!	Relax in the bath with your favourite bubble bath.	Listen to positive self-help tape of your choice.	Watch a comedy that makes you laugh.	Go out for dinner with a friend/partner. No GIN it's a depressant.	Watch TV and divert mental energy away from your own problems.	Do whatever you want you deserve it!
Write in your diary 3 positive things about your day, and a summary of your day.	Write in your diary 3 positive things about your day, and a summary of your day.	Write in your diary 3 positive things about your day, and a summary of your day.	Write in your diary 3 positive things about your day, and a summary of your day.	Write in your diary 3 positive things about your day, and a summary of your day.	Write in your diary 3 positive things about your day, and a summary of your day.	Write in your diary 3 positive things about your day, and a summary of your day.

A lot of people describe feeling numb whilst taking prescribed antidepressants. It seems to be one of the side-effects.

All medical drugs have side-effects, no matter what we are told to the contrary and antidepressants are no exception. Just take a look at the box and at the pages of disclaimers and side-effects in the small print stuffed in the box alongside the drugs.

One possible side-effect is euphoria. On seeing this, you might think, 'Really – get me some of those'. If you read on, another side-effect is suicidal tendencies. Is the rare possible side-effect of euphoria worth the possible side-effect of suicidal tendencies? That is a decision you have to make if you're allowed to make it yourself. I wasn't.

All drugs are foreign substances, designed to interfere with or change what is going on in your body. Antidepressants are no exception. If you are lucky they help the problem with few side-effects. If you are not so lucky they may cover up symptoms but not put right the original problem. I must have been very unlucky as not only did they not help my Depression but I had lots of horrible side-effects.

The doctors and my husband argued with me that the antidepressants were working and that I was worse when I wasn't taking medication but I couldn't remember ever feeling worse.

Prozac is the antidepressant that we have probably all heard of. I remember it being heralded as the 'wonder drug' treatment for depression. What wasn't reported was that it can cause anxiety and agitation, as well as insomnia and bizarre dreams, in a large percentage of patients and that it can also cause hypoglycaemia with anxiety, chills, cold sweats, confusion, weakness and other symptoms of low blood sugar.

Prozac was the first antidepressant that I was prescribed. I knew nothing about depression or antidepressants when I was first diagnosed. Prozac's (fluoxetine) reputation preceded it so I didn't protest at taking it (it's about the only one I didn't protest at taking!). Not that I was in any fit state to protest at that time but I wish that I had as when I started taking it I felt as if I had all of the above side-effects at the same time but definitely none of the benefits of an antidepressant.

I remember feeling 'off the wall' when I was taking it. I remember feeling like I was floating down the stairs. The ground didn't feel real beneath my feet. My head was dancing. It may sound great and I know that some people pay a lot of money for that feeling but it was truly a dreadful feeling for me. Everything felt surreal. I wanted to stop taking it as soon as possible. I felt dreadful.

The next antidepressant the doctor prescribed was olanzapine (Zyprexa). I was convinced that this drug was responsible for my initial considerable weight gain and so refused to take it. My diet and lack of exercise definitely didn't help but I wasn't going to let antidepressants add to it! Prozac did not perform the miracle I was expecting and had read about and now olanzapine was diminishing my faith in antidepressants. My husband thought that my mood had improved since I had started taking olanzapine and suggested that 'we' could deal with the weight gain later. I felt quite sure that there would have been no 'we' involved in 'dealing with the weight gain later' and refused to take it any more.

NEXT!......

So I moved onto venlafaxine (Effexor). I was sure this drug exacerbated my weight gain and the doctor confirmed this was one of the substantial side-effects along with: Loss of short to medium term memory; loss of drive; ambition and personal motivation; deterioration in eyesight and sexual dysfunction. I had no libido whilst on antidepressants but I never knew if it was my drugs or my Depression that caused this. I had my confirmation about my 'substantial weight gain' so no surprise when not another venlafaxine tablet passed my lips.

Thereafter I refused to take anything associated with weight gain. So I was prescribed Seroxat (paroxetine). My prescription coincided with negative reports in the press that this drug caused suicidal tendencies, a red flag for me. My doctor appropriately took me off it immediately.

As if my Depression wasn't bad enough, the doctor was now telling me that the drugs they were giving me could trigger reactions that cause my Depression to worsen. There is a lot of scientific research about the connection between suicide, violence and the use of psychiatric drugs. I was uncharacteristically quite violent too while I was depressed but I'm not sure if that was the sheer frustration at being ill or as a result of the drugs. I prefer to blame the drugs!

If at first you don't succeed, try, try trazodine (Molipaxin)!

I complained that I didn't think trazodine was working but no one was listening so I decided to take it upon myself to suddenly stop taking it without telling anyone. Big mistake!

I didn't think it was possible to feel any lower but stopping taking my medication certainly changed my mind on that one. My mood crashed terribly.

My husband noticed that my state had considerably worsened and asked me if I was still taking my medication. Eventually he dragged the truth out of me. He wasn't happy, I can tell you.

He dragged me back to the doctor for yet another change of antidepressant after explaining to the doctor that the reason I had stopped taking it was because I didn't think it was making any difference. This was my argument against taking all my antidepressants. It was my complaints against the side-effects that varied. I was convinced that the drugs were highly toxic and poisoning my body and that they weren't working anyway!

While they do say antidepressants are not addictive, it is still not advisable to stop taking any drug without medical supervision. They may not be addictive in the sense that you don't need to keep increasing the dose to get the same effect and you won't crave them if you stop taking them but it is known[5] that up to a third of people who stop taking SSRIs and SNRIs have withdrawal symptoms like stomach upsets, flu like symptoms, anxiety, dizziness, vivid dreams or

[5] according to The Royal College of Psychiatrists (RCPSYCH)

sensations in the body that feel like electric shocks. I felt worse than I had EVER felt.

I started taking trazodine again. From that day on, my husband would supervise my medication.

Even under his supervision, I used to pretend that I had swallowed them by holding them under my tongue until he had gone. Looking back, I cannot believe how deceitful I was. My poor husband was trying to help me. I was leading him a merry dance. I didn't think I was capable of such deceit. I know I was desperate. I was desperately depressed and I was desperate to stop taking medication that I didn't think was doing me any good.

My husband became worried at no improvement in my almost manic highs and debilitating lows.

We went back to the doctors again. This time I was prescribed the last letter of the alphabet, Zyban. That didn't work either.

So they decided to put me on tried and tested old favourite, lithium. Having been around since the Second WW lithium is prescribed as a last resort when none of the more modern antidepressants prove to be effective. Lithium's major disadvantage is the amount of side-effects it has and the need it has for weekly blood tests and close monitoring to measure the correct level in the blood. Did I mention I am terrified of injections? I really hate them. I usually faint actually. It is pure fear. What a wimp!

I used to skip my appointments for the blood tests due to my fear and at one point as a consequence of not having the level of lithium checked, I had too much lithium in my blood and was shaking so badly that I could hardly hold a cup. That was a major blow to my favourite, and indeed only, pastime when I was ill of sitting in cafes and drinking coffee (and eating chocolate muffins!). It was so embarrassing. This really upset my father. His daughter who had always been so positive and upbeat and happy was now reduced to a jabbering wreck.

This really disturbed me to the extent that I decided to have my body analysed by a professional QXCI expert to see if I was being poisoned as I suspected. This system[6] said that my body was fighting a 'toxinous' herb called lithium. The fact that it even detected the drug that I was taking frightened me. Here was my confirmation that my body was being poisoned. That was it, no more lithium for me.

In light of my inability to turn up for appointments for blood tests and my fear of 'being poisoned' by lithium the doctors reviewed my medication again. They were reluctant to take me off lithium due to its effectiveness in treating depression and wanted to reduce the dose and put me on Depakote (divalproex sodium) as well. I refused to take two lots of medication (goodness, there I go again with my attitude. I'd never been as awkward in my life before) and as I did not want to take lithium any more, I only agreed to take Depakote if they would wean me off the lithium. My doctor grudgingly agreed if I agreed to come off the lithium gradually and under his supervision. It was a deal.

---

[6] QXCI is a health assessment that was originally developed by NASA to check the health of astronauts.

I continued to feel absolutely dreadful and several months later I went back to the doctor of my own accord to ask why none of these antidepressants seemed to be making any difference.

He explained that Depakote was really to monitor my highs. 'What highs?' I exclaimed, rather too loudly. Pardon me for appearing obnoxious but from where I was sitting, I wasn't having any highs. I was feeling extremely low. My husband disagreed. He saw my excessive spending (explained later) as a manifestation of my manic highs.

"I need something to monitor the lows!" I pleaded tears streaming down my face. So I was prescribed lamotrigine to take alongside the Depakote. This way hopefully the Depakote could keep my highs in check (they must have been so high that they were off my radar as I hadn't noticed any highs for a long time!) and the lamotrigine (Lamictal) could monitor my lows.

This time, I reacted so badly that my whole body erupted in painful hives in the form of a full body rash. I had to stop and seek medical help in the middle of the night on the motorway on the way from Scotland to Nottingham to supposedly help my sick sister. It resulted in my being in bed ill for days. I wasn't much help to my sister and as always she was very understanding despite being very ill herself with chemotherapy treatment for breast cancer.

Finally the doctor then replaced lamotrigine with Seroquel (quetiapine). This was to be the medication that I stayed on until I stopped taking antidepressants. I still didn't feel any difference but at least I had minimal side-effects so I decided to 'give my doctor a break' and 'I put up and shut up'.

I personally was much more receptive to talking therapy for my Depression which I felt was helping me. You may not be surprised to hear that I didn't object to that at all. I think that my doctors were surprised!

I continued to explain and plead with my psychiatrist and doctor that apart from the physical pain I experienced from the side-effects of the anti-depressants, I wasn't feeling much else. After almost 10 years of taking antidepressants eventually I begged my psychiatrist to take me off them which he did grudgingly under his watchful eye. Secretly I think that he must have been very relieved to put away his A-Z of antidepressants! He did however make me promise to take a very good omega-3 every day which I still do.

ALTERNATIVE HAPPY PILLS

- **Omega-3**

Clinical studies have proven the benefit of omega-3 fish oil in depression and in particular, the long chain fatty acid known as EPA (eicosapentaenoic acid) which is the purest form.

I can honestly say for me there was a difference between ordinary omega-3 and the EPA version. My friend's research paid off as she told me about 'Vegepa' omega-3 fish oil supplements with EPA and Evening Primrose oil which are pharmaceutical grade supplements. She swears by them. I swear by them too now. I always trust this friend if she recommends anything to me (and wish she'd recommend more things to help me sort my life out).

Vegepa is excellent and I really feel the difference. It's been recommended by many reputable sources in scientific journals and by the world's leading medical researchers and clinicians. Professor Puri recommends it in his book 'the natural way to beat depression - The groundbreaking discovery of EPA to change your life'.

- **Multivitamins**

I also started taking multivitamin supplements, in particular vitamins B6, B9 and B12, and zinc that I have been told by nutritionists and have read help in the treatment of depression; magnesium for anxiety.

- **Herbal remedies**

Herbal or homeopathic remedies are at least in general sympathetic to the body and have good side-effects. Filisa and St John's Wort are for some people as effective against depression as other modern medication.

Filisa - has no contraindications and can be taken alongside antidepressants or on its own. Many people have found that Filisa works very well for them. It worked for me.

St John's Wort - Be careful how you use it as it can cause multiple drug interactions with some drugs including hormonal contraception.

Bach remedies - are plant based remedies directed at a particular characteristic or emotional state. Rescue Remedy is probably the best known Bach Flower remedy. As its name suggests it is a remedy to deal with emergencies and crises.

I once sneaked a few drops of Rescue Bach Flower Remedy into my friends' cups of tea when they were staying with me when they were having a serious argument about getting divorced and it seemed to calm them down pretty quickly after they drank their tea. Of course it could have been the tea! Don't underestimate the power of natural remedies. Don't knock anything until you've tried it!

- **Supplements**

SAM-e has gained popularity in recent years and has been shown in clinical trials to be as effective as standard antidepressant medication with many fewer side-effects. Tryptophan, an essential amino acid, is the precursor to the happy hormone serotonin. Tryptophan and 5-HTP dietary supplements have also been used as natural antidepressants. 5-HTP is naturally found in turkey, chicken, fish, beans and eggs, bananas and avocado, and is vital for the production of serotonin so I eat plenty of those too.

I tried the whole lot, together. I would rather have taken anything and everything than my prescribed meds. My doctors must have been very frustrated with me along with my husband. While herbal medicines and remedies are natural, they can also be very potent and powerful which is good as it means that they work but as such they should still be respected and not be taken while taking other medication without consulting your doctor.

Studies show that in most cases it is the depression that causes the chemical imbalance and not the chemical imbalance that causes the depression. So if the depression is causing your chemical imbalance, the antidepressant is treating the symptom and not the cause.

My Depression was triggered by circumstances. The doctors call it 'exogenous' depression or 'reactive' depression. It was my negative thinking that made me depressed and my Depression that caused the chemical imbalance and not the other way round.

I was depressed for a long time about my situation and didn't see a way out. I did all the things that were feeding the depression like thinking negatively and introspectively and ruminating for days, weeks and months on end in my bed. No wonder the black dog grew so big!

Because I was depressed for so long the chemical balance in my brain did change and I was treated with medication to try to lift my mood enough to be receptive to therapy to help me to deal with my reaction to those circumstances and to learn the skills to react differently in the future.

It is important to note that antidepressants do not work like a headache tablet or a tranquilliser. They do not work if administered like a headache tablet as and when you need it. To be effective they be taken consistently as prescribed by your doctor. I have a friend who tried to use them like a headache tablet unsuccessfully. Don't forget when you stop them they don't start to work overnight so once you stop you'll have to wait for weeks again to feel any better.

It is also not advisable to take antidepressants without a prescription. Don't take a few packets of a friend's prescriptive antidepressants thinking that they will help you if they help your friend. The diagnosis of each patient, the prescription of an antidepressant and dosage is carefully chosen for each patient based on a long and complicated process that requires the knowledge of a professional. We are all wonderfully different, and what works for one person may not work for another.

I was never a very good advert for antidepressants so none of my friends ever asked for my many unused packets!

My husband was very worried (and who wouldn't be) when I started hearing my deceased mother talking to me and asking him if he could 'hear the numbers talking'. Very worrying! Apparently I was very specific about which numbers were talking. He has since recounted the numbers 95621. Very strange! And no they didn't win on the lottery either – in any combination. I think it is how many times he would have liked sex when I chose chocolate instead.

I have to say that I have no recollection of any of the numbers or voices talking, thank goodness. I heard very strange things, did very strange things and thought very strange things during my Depression.

Subsequently I was given tranquilisers to calm me down.

Tranquillisers are often prescribed to medicate mild agitation, edginess, everyday anxiety and sleeping problems. They **are** addictive and can have reverse effects by raising anxiety levels. Unfortunately this often leads patients to think that his or her nerves are getting worse and taking more.

The minor tranquillisers that receive publicity because of their abuse potential and their dangerous and lethal interaction with only moderate alcohol are Valium (diazepam), Xanax, Serax, Ativan (lorazepam), Klonopin, Librium, and Tranxene.

I got to the stage that I would not leave the house to do anything stressful (which was basically everything except shopping!) without a Valium or half a Valium. I could not even meet a friend for a coffee without one. I had no confidence. I was scared of making a fool of myself, of people thinking that I was stupid.

It got to the stage that I would write down a message word-for-word that I would leave on friends' answering machines when I knew they would be out, saying that I was OK but that I wouldn't be in touch for a while until I felt up to it. That would get me 'off the hook' of having to speak to anyone. I did not feel confident enough to have a spontaneous conversation.

I was convinced that I would be stuck for words, say the wrong thing, not be able to think of how to say what I really wanted to say, upsetting someone. My goodness, the smallest activity was a complete nightmare. The extremes I would go to, to avoid talking to people, seems unbelievable now and when I look back and remember these times, I realise how far I have come.

I set a totally unrealistic goal to complete an accountancy course, part of my quick fix to employment and financial security. Once again I set myself up for further depression but would not be told! I took a Valium every morning to get me through the course and if I forgot to take it before I left the house, I may as well have given up as, in my mind, I would not cope with the day.

I got my certificate but I have no idea how I managed it. I guess the Valium helped! My negative and distorted thinking preferred to believe that they gave me my certificate because they felt sorry for me. Now, in my rational frame of mind, I realise that it would not have done the London Business School's reputation any good to give people certificates if they didn't deserve them.

Most evenings I used to take a sedative to calm me down as I was always so agitated by the end of the day. I used to keep a bottle of sedatives in my handbag and a bottle by my bedside. A bottle of Rescue Remedy by Bach Flower Remedies is much less extreme and still seems to do the trick these days.

My husband understood my need for the sedatives and was always guided by the advice of the doctors but even he was concerned by my dependence on them and resorted to hiding them and giving me one when he thought it was necessary.

Looking back, I really cannot believe that life was like this. What kind of life is that?

Medication really did dominate my life.

I think the doctors think that if they take the feelings away, we'll be fine.

How many of us have been to our doctor and been prescribed pills? According to an article I read, 80% of doctors are too readily prescribing medication for depression and symptoms thereof. I can believe that.

At the time I thought I was destined to take antidepressants for the rest of my life. I certainly didn't want to be popping my pills for ever especially when I could see there was another way with therapy and herbal remedies.

Obviously, pills are necessary for a lot of medical illnesses. Surely treatment for depression is more likely to be successful if you find out why you feel depressed in the first place and put this right. Many of my friends have been prescribed antidepressants without getting to the crux of what is causing their Depression.

We all have our own story that has been shaped by family, background, circumstances, education and peers, etc. That's why the treatment for depression is different in each case. It is often easier for busy doctors to prescribe pills for immediate effect. We obviously all just want to feel better as quickly as possible. It's an all too familiar pattern. However this doesn't encourage or help us to change whatever it is in our lives that is causing our Depression. It just helps us to carry on with our old, obviously damaging, lifestyles and issues but cope a little better.

I do believe it is possible with the right therapy and therapist, combined with the correct medication you can get a solution that works for you. You can feel strong, empowered, and positive without needing to take drugs or take drugs for a long period of time.

There are lots of things you can do to lift your mood besides just popping pills and professional therapy (See chapters 'Therapy Begins at Home' and 'Therapy Man'). After all, therapy tends to be for an hour, once a week. Taking pills only takes up two or three minutes after each meal. What about the other 23 hours 51 minutes a day? Even a depressive cannot sleep for that long. How can anyone expect this to be a sufficient amount of dedicated time to get better? Use some of these spare hours wisely. Even if you work and have families you can find some more time, you are worth more than that. You commit more time than that to cutting your toe nails!

Don't discount antidepressants. They do have their place. Antidepressants are preferred for deep, often suicidal depression and can make patients less anxious. To see them as a temporary helping hand, a temporary emotional crutch can be invaluable. For many people, a short course of antidepressants can give them the lift that they need, to get them off the bottom of the well, onto the first step of the ladder, so that they feel resourceful enough to start some form of psychotherapy or counselling, or it can give them the little boost to deal with the little every day things that need to be done...in the short term. It does not take the place or alleviate the need for psychotherapy. It will work and you will become a fully functioning person again. This is not about a quick fix!

THE BLOODY WEIGHT GAIN!

The weight gain was definitely partly due to the antidepressants but my 'sloth' like existence wasn't helping.

When I finally admitted that I wasn't helping my weight gain by eating far too much of everything and doing absolutely nothing, I was so overweight that I had what looked like cellulite on my tummy. I was devastated. So I did what every woman in desperation does and phoned my beautician.

I ended up signing myself up for a course of 10 treatments of endermologie! After all if the F.D.A. and Advertising Standards Agency approve, it must work, right?! Endermologie is a rather radical treatment that involves climbing in to a full body stocking and having your body sucked and rolled by a contraption that very much resembles and feels like a vacuum cleaner suction pipe. It was rather uncomfortable. In fact I distinctly remember the odd nip but the 'No pain, no gain' principal kept me going back to complete the course. I believed that it would be like a course of antibiotics and if I didn't take the full course, it would not work. That too cost a fortune.

In fact most of the things I attempted to look and feel better ended up costing lots of money but they don't have to. The cellulite tummy is no more but I did do exactly what the beautician advised and combined the treatment with moderate exercise (moderate exercise is all I was capable of at that time), and a good(ish) diet. Isn't it funny how a lot of these fancy treatments advise doing that!?

Of course my diet wasn't helping my Depression. I was eating so much junk food. Fruit and vegetables were not high on my list of priorities. Coffee and biscuits and cakes and sweets were. I wasn't exactly nourishing my mind and body. In fact I was denying it anything anywhere near its natural state and depleting my body of its calcium reserves by drinking far too many fizzy drinks, mostly tonic water and worse still the tonic was to dilute the gin, which is widely known to be a depressant in itself! What did I expect?

I know what is good for me and what is bad for me but I didn't care. I didn't particularly like myself and that showed in the way I treated my body. I was abusing it with the junk that I was eating.

The words of my friend are imprinted on my brain even today: "PUT IT IN THE BIN. THE BIN WON'T PUT ON WEIGHT".

Easier said than done, I say. I had been using myself as the bin and it showed.

Another problem with the weight was that I did not know how to dress. I had always been slim and had worked hard in the gym to keep toned. Suddenly I ballooned and put on four stone and found myself having to buy size 16/18 clothes from 8/10. I had no idea what type of clothes to buy to make the most of myself. To be honest, for a long time, I wasn't interested in doing anything to make the most of myself but when I did care, my weight upset me very much and merely served to add another dimension to my Depression.

I felt totally invisible to everyone, particularly the opposite sex. But let's face it, I was dressing and acting invisible. I used to work really hard to find the drabbest outfit in my wardrobe, not make an effort with my hair and not wear any make up. Even the Hollywood celebrities look grim when they are trying to be invisible or 'incognito'. I've seen it in the magazines. If dressing down, a bad hair day and no make up can make them invisible, it's obviously going to work for me! I was making ME invisible.

There's a pattern here!

I know lots of really attractive larger women and men. They dress really well and look after the way they look, dress and act and they certainly aren't invisible.

We can all stew on how we are not beautiful enough, thin enough, sexy enough, and tall enough. Whatever your own issues are, it's very easy to stew on them. It's nice to stew on nice things too, like what a great chest we have, what lovely hair we have, what piercing blue eyes we have. Make the most of what we have. You might like yourself. Or is that what you're afraid of?

We might not know how to do that but someone out there does know. Go to the experts for advice. It does not have to cost the earth.

I didn't want to just wear black tracksuit bottoms or jeans with baggy black sweatshirts and fleeces. I was struggling to find clothes for my new weight. I felt like I was dressing a different person and I was too embarrassed to pick up nice clothes for fear of people laughing at me and wondering why I was bothering to spend money on clothes when I was so fat.

I had no one to go shopping with to help me. Most husbands hate shopping and lie anyway when you ask, 'Does my bum look big in this?' just so they can get home and watch the TV. It's certainly not how you want to spend a fun girlie weekend shopping for 'fat' clothes as shopping for 'fat' clothes isn't fun and shopping on my own for large, shapeless sacks just fuelled my low mood. For a start the fact that everything I picked up was black, I was asking for trouble.

That is when I discovered my personal shopper. I promise you that I have not looked back since. You do not pay for the services of the personal shopper in the big stores. You just pay for the items of clothing you buy. Most of the larger retail outlets have personal shoppers now.

I'm sure that they are all lovely as their job is to make people feel and look good. I am very pleased that I hooked up with the personal shopper I did when I called the shop. We hit it off in an instant. Actually, I defy anyone not to hit it off with Emma. She is vivacious, down to earth and has a wicked sense of humour, not to mention beautiful. I thought that that would intimidate me but she is such a beautiful person that I could not possibly have felt anything other than comfortable with her. She brought me complementary coffee and biscuits that helped the experience get off to a good start!

We then did the inevitable discussion of 'best' and 'worst' bits whilst looking in the mirror but it wasn't anything like as degrading or awful as Trinny and Susannah make it look and I had my coffee and biscuits to fall back on. It was actually real fun.

Emma and I then went out on to the shop floor together to peruse the collections available to the 'larger woman'. She knew exactly where to look, what to pick up, what would suit me and what colours would flatter the most (surprisingly not black as we all insist on wearing when we feel the bulge) and how to bring out my best features even though I didn't think that I currently had any! We seemed to laugh the whole time.

Then we went back to the dressing room to try everything on. I could not believe the results. I could not believe that I was looking at me in the mirror. I did not look like the fat elephant that I felt like. I actually thought that I looked 'quite' attractive. If Emma hadn't made it such fun, I think that I would have been in tears as I could not believe what I was looking at in the mirror. I felt good. I looked good.

I lost almost four stone in a year and a half. Looking good even at a size 16/18 gave me the will and the determination to try to lose weight by exercising and eating healthily. Emma has seen me go from a size 16/18 to a size 8/10 and never fails to make me feel and look wonderful. The process of looking good along the way from 14 stone to 10 stone gave me the incentive to carry on and never to give up.

You also get to feel like a celebrity for the session and have one on one attention which can't fail to make you feel good.

If I have an important occasion or event and I need something new, she knows exactly what will fit and suit me without my being there to try it on and will just send it out to me if I cannot get in or will put it to one side for me until I can get in to try it on.

You do not have to buy everything your personal shopper recommends and you do not have to use a personal shopper all the time. You can have the fun of shopping on your own or with friends but a personal shopper can help you to learn what to look for.

We all have our 'safe, tried and tested' look that gets us the compliments 'Oh, you look nice'. We tend to get stuck with that look and rarely venture beyond it whereas someone else can visualise you looking fantastic in a completely different look.

Just visualise how it would feel to have someone say 'Wow, you look gorgeous'.

We do it with hairstyles all the time (particularly when we are fresh out of a relationship!). Why not change your fashion style as well and change the whole package? It's a great feeling. Try it.

I even started experimenting with make up again.

I went for free makeovers at make up counters in the large stores. You do not even have to buy anything. Often you are so pleased with the results that you want to buy that cheeky pink lipstick or 'to die for' eye shadow. They know that. It is always a possible sale for them and is part of their job to demonstrate what their product can do.

I got really friendly with one counter and used to go in for my make up to be done before I went out in the evening. I felt great. You feel like you have your own make up artist. You feel special, pampered and confident.

I've been so often that I know how to do it myself now and I can change my look to suit my mood (always good of course!), occasion and outfit.

It is important to feel good. When a woman walks in to a room, she doesn't look at the men first, she looks at the women to weigh up the competition. She compares herself to the other women in the room. Then she looks at the men. Many of my male friends admit that they do that too (look at the other men that is!)

I felt fat and I didn't feel good though and was trying to buy things to make me feel good. I bought things to make me look better and I bought things to make me feel better that didn't depend on my weight. I even went out and bought lots of pairs of glasses to try to change the shape of my face and tried coloured contact lenses to change the 'boring' colour of my eyes. I cannot believe now that I disliked myself so much that I didn't even like the colour of my eyes!

Both my husband and I ended up with very spotty complexions during my Depression that I never dreamed I would have to deal with again after adolescence. It was so annoying. It got so bad that I stopped wearing make up to see if that helped. I didn't really feel attractive enough to wear make up anyway and to be honest just used my spots as an excuse. So not only was I fat, I was spotty too!

I went for loads of facials but the main culprit of my weight and my spots was my diet, lack of exercise and the toxins in my body from my medication concoction. I am sure that my husband's spots were due to the stress of my illness and its repercussions.

Given that I was feeling and looking so dreadful, I needed some positive affirmations about me. Not affirmations that I didn't look fat because I knew that I did and I would not have believed those kinds of compliments anyway. I always fixated on the negatives and the insults. When you are down, you don't even hear the compliments. I thought that friends and family were lying when they said that I looked well.

When I feel bad about a particular aspect of myself I don't want compliments that contradict that aspect that I know to be ugly, fat, too big or too small. I need encouragement that I am improving and doing better. When I felt and was fat, I didn't want to be told that I didn't look fat because I knew that I did look fat. I did like it when I was asked if I'd lost weight because that told me that people weren't denying that I was overweight but that they could tell that I was doing something about it.

We all need encouragement. Just remember how much better you feel when someone says something positive to you. Let the compliment in. Just learn to say thank you. That lets it in and allows you to feel better.

My husband was so mad with me and my spending and my behaviour that I am sure he found it impossible to think of anything positive to say and his negative comment of the day, usually to do with my spending, would send me to my bed.

It actually became a joke that when I used to ask for a compliment (he never volunteered them), I used to plead, “Say something nice to me” and he used to respond, “You’re not ugly”. He’d given up with normal compliments. It was the only compliment he felt that I wouldn’t reject. It always made me laugh.

Exercise had always made me feel good in the past but I did not have much energy so I walked a lot with my dog. Don’t get me wrong, a lot of the time I was looking for the next cliff to jump off. I did it regularly if it wasn’t raining or too windy as I am a fair-weather everything obviously.

I got my dog when I was depressed but not to lose weight. I got her because I felt that a loving dog would help my Depression. Firstly I knew that stroking her would help as they say stroking a dog reduces stress. I didn’t think about the result of having a small goal to look forward to getting out of bed for and to walking by the sea with her which were also very good for lifting my mood.

It was because she was such a naughty dog and I had no control over her that I used to do a lot of running as I would end up chasing after her as she would always run off even when I called her back. She had a lot of energy and as I got more energy I started to run with her (always more like after her!) and we both benefited as she released her pent up tension and became more well behaved as a result and I got fitter and lost weight and my mood lifted and I became more well behaved as a result too! It was a win win situation for us both. I like those situations. They don't happen very often. They definitely don't happen often enough do they?

I started to go to yoga because I had read that it was a good all rounder for depression and anxiety as it combines breathing, meditation and the poses and of course it helped that it was all the rage again and all the celebs were doing it. So I went out and bought the yoga mat and bag and the rest of the kit. I was the novice sportsman with all the right gear but no clue as to what I was doing and stuck out like a sore thumb. I couldn't even touch my toes but luckily the teacher suspected that when I turned up looking like I did! I went with a friend who was also going through a difficult time with her ex-husband at the time. I was dreading being in a room full of bendy, skinny people but in fact it turned out to be a class of very normal people who all seemed to be going through a tough time so we all got on very well together.

My friend and I used to make a morning of it and go for a coffee afterwards. We wanted a cake but couldn't as she was trying to lose her post baby weight and I was trying to lose my post 'stuffing my face' weight, so we used to compromise and have half a cake each.

My sisters-in-law went beyond the call of duty to help me lose weight. They would often call for me to walk the dogs together and even tried ballet with me to do something different as I did not have the energy to 'pump it up' in the gym but I couldn't be serious in the class at the sight of my sisters-in-law and myself in the mirror jumping around like fairies. Some people looked very elegant jumping around but we didn't, so that was the end of the ballet classes.

You don't know unless you try.

I strongly recommend Pilates too. It is fantastic for developing core muscles and firming that tummy and everything else actually. It is a great workout and manageable at all levels of fitness and energy and age. I have been doing it since I had absolutely no energy and am still doing it and getting great results since getting my energy back.

You may think that a personal trainer is extravagant but I had absolutely no motivation to get myself out there to do anything. Having someone knock on my door to force me to go out for a walk or a run and give me company and encouragement, really helped me and my trainer was no more expensive than a gym membership would cost me and my training was personally geared to me and MY MOODS.

How many times have you found £60 per month bleeding out of your bank account for a gym membership that you never use because you cannot get yourself motivated? I was guaranteed a workout every week for the same cost as my gym membership that I wasn't using.

I just could not face going in to a gym full of fit people all looking fantastic and talking the annoying positive talk 'I did 30 minutes on the running machine and 100 sit ups'. It just would have driven me right back out again as I was feeling totally 'shit' about myself.

When I felt more energised and had progressed from walking quickly to power walking we then started running and he even started talking about the possibility of a half marathon. You notice, I say, he talked about it and I stress the word POSSIBILITY. It is true, I would like to run a half marathon one day but for the moment it remains just that; i.e. One Day.

Sometimes he used to come to the door and I would answer in tears that I couldn't go out today as I was having a particularly bad day and that was fine. He has always been very understanding. At that time he was training to become an instructor of Pilates and wanted to film one of our Pilates sessions as a case study but I used to get so frustrated with myself that my bad language (that my father blames on my city life!) would not have been acceptable for his case study and he had to find somebody else! He finds my self-criticism very funny and I have to admit that I do spend a lot of time laughing but that's good too[7].

I began to notice that the more I exercised and the more I made an effort with my make up and clothes, the less I was craving junk food, sweets and cakes. I didn't do this consciously. It would sound much more deserved if I had. Mind you, the exercise wasn't 'a walk in the park' so I would like to take some credit for it! But it was

---

[7] I found my personal trainer by asking at my local gym but your local telephone directory is always a good bet or the web.

always fun so I looked forward to it and the results were definitely worth it.

I've always known that the subconscious mind is much more powerful than the conscious mind because it is more suggestible and less doubting than the conscious mind as it hasn't been affected by life experiences. People say that hypnosis is a lazy way to do things but it seems an obvious way to me. There aren't many shortcuts in life that work as well as the long way round. I compare it to learning. If you were given the choice to learn the easy way or the hard way, why wouldn't you choose the easy way? It makes total sense to me.

Marisa Peer[8], my hypnotherapist, offered to hypnotise me to lose weight and sent me away with some hypnosis CDs to listen to. I had never been hypnotised before. I'd seen people being hypnotised on the television and I'd seen Marisa hypnotising people on the television but I wasn't sure if I wanted to be hypnotised myself.

I think my concern was not being in control of the situation and not understanding the process but I was very unhappy with my weight and for a long time had not been in the frame of mind to do anything productive enough about it to make a difference on my own so I accepted her offer.

It was a strange (in the sense that everything is strange until you've done it once) yet wonderful experience. I felt like I was entering a deep sleep as Marisa's soothing voice led me down and counted me down 10 steps. I don't remember getting to the bottom actually

---

[8] Author of 'You Can Be Thin' and 'Ultimate Confidence'.

but I do remember feeling deeply relaxed and very comfortable and contented as if I had a smile on my face. I felt fully conscious but also remember that I couldn't open my eyes and remember consciously trying to do so. That's about all I have ever been able to recall about the hypnotherapy sessions themselves but afterwards I felt like I had woken from a perfect deep sleep. I felt a bit drowsy for 20 minutes or so and then wonderfully free of burden for the rest of the day. Even if it hadn't worked it would have been a wonderful experience but it did work for me. My tastes began to change and my cravings disappeared.

It was like the slippery slope in reverse. It felt good. It was as if my mind liked what was happening to my body and it wanted to follow suit. I had been making half-hearted efforts for months to lose weight by drinking pints of various types of slimming tea and eating low calorie chocolate bars instead of every other type of chocolate but now everything was beginning to fall into place. After what seemed to have been a really hard slog for a really long time I seemed to suddenly be seeing big results. It really did seem to happen all of a sudden.

I bought more fresh fruit and vegetables and actually enjoyed them. We all like results and get incentivised by them and I was seeing results.

I really put my weight loss down to a combination of all these things but mainly following a healthy diet (There's a chapter on diet to come), exercise, walking my dog and hypnotherapy.

Exercise and diet are paramount to good mental health. You need to find the right healthy diet and exercise for you.

With exercise I would recommend choosing things that you enjoy doing so that you keep doing them. It's the same principle for food, find what you like to eat that is good for you. Don't be afraid to try new things. You may surprise yourself! With exercise I was worse than I could ever have dreamed at some things and better than I could ever have dreamed at others.

Similarly a healthy diet that is recommended to you may not be to your taste. Have fun finding what works for you.

WHY AM I DEPRESSED?

"I'm not the kind of person who gets depressed." This was my constant argument with my dad, my husband and my doctors. But my father said something to me that made me laugh. 'One in four people is unbalanced. Look at your three closest friends. If it's not them, it must be you!' Thanks for that, dad! He's probably right though.

I'd never even contemplated that I could possibly be depressed. I didn't know what depression was. I did not understand the term.

That was probably part of the problem. I did not know what the problem was and in fact when my husband finally got me to the doctor after a year of dramatic deterioration in my physical and mental state, the initial prognosis was 'physical and mental exhaustion'.

It should not have come as any surprise really. I was getting up at 4am most mornings, commuting, overworking, never leaving the office before 9pm, going to the gym, cleaning the house too often and well before it had chance to look lived in and not eating. What did I expect? Other people thought my behaviour on the surface to be admirable. You could say that sounds great but it was completely obsessive and was a way of avoiding confronting difficult feelings.

Another thing I was possibly dealing with was FEAR. My fear of not being "enough". I feared failing and making mistakes. We all make mistakes along the way but we are only human and I've learned so much from my mistakes, I'm now not shy of making a few more! As my friend says, 'Laugh at yourself and your mistakes. Everybody else does!' I'm sure she doesn't mean that they are all laughing at me! I think it sounds like a good idea. Why should it just be everyone else's fun? Learning to laugh at yourself is a great turning point.

Other people fear being alone and it makes them love unsuitables.

People fear that they won't be loved. We all want and indeed need to be loved and to know that we are cared for. We're all in search of that from birth. Unfortunately, not everyone is handed the 'Fairytale'. In fact very few of us are. That's just a fact of life. This fear often drives us beyond our means and we struggle on when we should acknowledge that we are struggling and get out and do something about it.

Depression Can Be Fun

Depressives are very good at covering up our true feelings. We're certainly great actors when it comes to putting on an act if we want to. We are so good at it that even our closest family and friends don't know that we are depressed. This didn't help my illness or my husband. A lot of my friends didn't believe that I was so ill because of my great acting skills and thought that he was exaggerating. By acting fine in front of them I actually denied him their support which he really could have done with at such a difficult time. It was such hard work to try to act as if I was fine and used to leave me absolutely drained and even more depressed. The only time I used to feel able to be myself and show and let out how I felt was at home because I felt so ashamed and embarrassed about my Depression. That meant that the only person who saw how ill I really was, was my husband.

Denial went on for a long time. I struggled on for a year before my husband persuaded me to go to the doctor.

There can be many causes of depression and it's ageless. It's certainly not discriminatory or forgiving. It doesn't care who it sweeps up along its way.

Even the experts don't fully understand depression and the brain so why should we as total laymen be expected to know and understand why we are depressed?

Depression has existed for ever and every generation had its own demands.

Life has changed since 1940's Britain. We have different issues, different fears, different aspirations and different pressures. Changes in society mean that our basic needs for companionship, healthy goals, responsibility, connection to others and meaning are not automatically met. We have more money and more choice but we are definitely not happier.

If we learned to appreciate life like our grandparents did, like that crocheted blanket or hand me down dress, everything would be fine but our generation is reprogrammed to earn to buy happiness. Happiness is mainly seen financially. So the vicious circle continues.

We have come to think, as a society, that money can buy everything but it can't. It can't seem to buy happiness. Just look around. Many of the wealthiest people in our world are the people that are the most unhappy.

In our grandmother's day women could feel isolated, and undervalued. The husband and normally the breadwinner often felt overburdened with having to singularly provide for his family but these difficulties were often lessened because families supported each other much more. People were different then. They were more content with their lives and their 'lot'. Modern materialism hadn't taken hold yet.

Some husbands are finding themselves as house husbands and in a very similar role to our grandmothers. Men must be confused at their changing role just as much as women who go out to work and are no longer just a housewife and mother. Since time began, the man has been the hunter/provider and the woman has been the protector and hoarder. My brother thinks that this evolution explains a woman's need to shop to have lots of things around her and men like Porsche 911 Carrera 4S's because they don't have plumage and lions' mains to impress their females in mating season. What is happening today is going against thousands of years of evolution. Society has changed but we haven't.

I often think that there is no wonder that so many people have 'mental problems' because we are trying to change the 'rules' that have been in place since Adam and Eve. How can we expect our minds and bodies to catch up when we are trying to change in 50 years what we have always known and the world has always been?

The root of depression can be felt as early as childhood and school. We have to choose what we want to study as young teenagers and it could affect the rest of our life. I remember feeling fearful that this decision could mean failure in later life if I made the wrong decision.

I worked to earn enough money to provide for my family and to avoid losing our income and at the end it was not because I wanted to.

I spent too much time worrying about what could go wrong and defending my actions.

What can worrying about the past and future achieve? It's so much better to enjoy the present and look forward to the future. Worry changes nothing. It is a waste of your time and energy. It does burn calories apparently. If worrying can burn calories, it tells you how stressful it is on the body.

Worry leads to stress, anxiety, hyperactivity, burnout and depression which then affect all areas of our life.

Our consumerist society encourages us to acquire things that are expensive, beautiful, and exciting.

Once I was ill, I tried to fill the gap left in my meaningless life with instant gratification. Hence the obsessive shopping hysteria and the term 'retail therapy' that now exists. In the end, though, I didn't find this constant instant gratification satisfying. It was just a temporary fix. It also amounted to a large debt and of course added to the depression.

I used to still feel tired when I woke up in the morning, had to force myself to get out of bed, drag myself through the day, never had enough energy or drive to do what I had to do, sometimes I'd even end up not able to go to work or run the home or I'd spend a lot of the day crying or sleeping and going to bed as early as I could. In effect I used to get up to go to bed.

I constantly used to push myself. I became exhausted, even physically ill. But the fear of having my own inadequacy confirmed kept me going. Inadequacy and disappointment in oneself creates depressed feelings, intensified by exhaustion.

Some people think that if they are having problems in their personal lives it automatically means that they can't be successful in any area of their lives. This is certainly not true and can lead to feelings of depression.

Some people have low self-esteem or don't like themselves and feel that they don't deserve the good things in life or to be happy. Low self-esteem and this type of thinking can lead to depression or can be caused by depression.

Some people are over cynical about life and prospects for change or they believe that this is all there is and it's stupid to expect more. This can result in depression.

On the other hand, there is the saying 'If you don't expect too much in life, you won't be disappointed and everything else is a bonus.'

It's important to do the things in life that need to be done but it is even more important to give ourselves time to reflect on us and re-energise. We allow ourselves little time to look at our lives to understand why we are not happy, why our emotional needs are not being met, how we could use our strengths and talents in a healthy and balanced way and what we want out of life. My brother summed this up rather well I thought when he said: "I don't have time to scratch my arse, never mind figure out what is wrong with my life". I couldn't have put it better myself but I wouldn't necessarily have put it like that!

We confuse hard work with suffering and do not know when to get out and give up. The result is inevitable really.

Too much stress and lack of or inability to sleep can take you into a very depressive state. There is good stress and bad stress. We all know the difference from the buzz we get from good stress and the physical and emotional side-effects (exhaustion, anxiety, irritability, insomnia, blood pressure problems, stomach problems and heart palpitations) we get from bad stress. We all know how difficult it is to think and function normally without sleep.

Some women suffer from depression following childbirth, often related to hormonal changes or, as my sister pointed out, from being totally 'knackered!'

For some, depression is triggered by a trauma such as the death of a loved one, an illness, accident or the loss of a valued job or the end of a relationship. Pain of loss through death or the end of a relationship is the hard feeling of grief. Extended grieving or not allowing ourselves time to grieve can cause depression. Grief is normal and healthy and temporary but becomes depression when it lasts well past the time that you would expect to start recovering from grief. We must grieve and let ourselves grieve at the time to avoid later depression. If we don't, we leave ourselves vulnerable to the debilitating effects of delayed grief in the form of depression when something else in our lives acts as the catalyst to unleash a box full of old emotions that then totally overwhelm us. Maybe this also had something to do with my Depression. My way of dealing with my mother's death was to imagine that she had gone away to have cosmetic surgery! (don't ask me why?). Unfortunately none of us get lessons in grieving. Well intended suggestions from friends and family to 'cheer up' and 'try to put it behind you' can be counterproductive. Grief is a natural form of depression that no doctor, drug or psychic for that matter can take away. Time is often the best healer. It sucks but it is true.

My doctors said I could have been prone to depression from birth due to several people in my family suffering from depression. Some experts say that depression can be genetic. More about that later. There are lots of 'can bes' and 'maybes' in this world and I do believe that some people are more sensitive, more prone to pushing themselves too hard, more needing to prove themselves or please others due to either their make-up or their background or upbringing etc and all of these things can trigger or lead to depression.

The doctors also told me that when you have suffered from depression once, you are more vulnerable to suffer another bout. On the one hand I wish they wouldn't say that because I think one can almost talk oneself into that 'other bout' with such knowledge or live in fear of it happening again. On the other hand it does encourage one to be on the 'lookout' for warning signs along that slippery slope back there. So I guess as with everything in this life, it's six of one and half a dozen of the other.

I feel sure that by knowing and changing what made me ill I can certainly lessen the likelihood of it happening again.

I always tried to do too much. I found it hard to say no to people, to cut back or ask for help and I needed to be everything to everybody.

I also used to take responsibility for things over which I had little or no control.

Can you relate to this? I felt guilty over a birthday party that I organised that was ruined by unexpected rain. We all know that there is little one can do about the weather, particularly in the UK! My husband who is Scottish always says, "If you don't like the weather, wait 10 minutes and it will change". Unfortunately it didn't that day. It rained ALL day. Funny how I didn't praise the things I did well like when it was sunny all day and the party went well! If you insist on taking the credit for the negative outcomes, at least be consistent and take the credit for the positive outcomes!

People pleasers often suffer from depression. I fall into this category. We try to please everyone and the burden becomes too much for us. We try to be everything to everyone. We often end up offending or hurting people we care about unintentionally because we try to do too much for too many people and spread ourselves too thinly and end up leaving others feeling as if we haven't given enough. I am only now learning to prioritise and plan. I find it hard but it's getting easier and I like the results.

High achievers set themselves up for depression. I am a high achiever. We set unrealistic goals. Our criteria for happiness and success are extreme and largely unrealistic. 'I will only be happy or successful when I have the respect and approval of all the people I work with; when I'm rich; when I .... (You get the picture!)'.

I have learned that I will probably always set myself such targets, but I am learning that I can be happy if I am doing well, I am appreciated and have a happy balanced work and social life.

Why limit your happiness or success in life to huge achievements? You risk failure and depression. If you do achieve them, that is absolutely fantastic.

I am not saying don't have goals and dreams, in fact I think that they are important antidotes to depression. I have found it is much better and healthier to set realistic goals even if it's just to get up out of bed in the morning. If you have a goal, aim for it. If you have a dream, keep dreaming it. Just make them realistic, rewarded, motivated, stimulated and reinforced and keep depression alienated. I am learning to re-evaluate what achievement is and set myself more realistic goals.

I used to focus only on long term goals which seemed so far off and impossible to reach.

I also had abstract goals: to be top of the class both at school and at work, be happy, be a good partner and eventually a good parent. This seemed overwhelming and unobtainable because the steps that led to those goals were not clear.

I learned to set short term goals and redefine each goal into smaller chunks which would ultimately lead to the abstract goals I mentioned earlier. The journey to the goal can be as enjoyable and rewarding as the goal itself. My sister-in-law refers to "TATTs" or Tiny Achievable Tickable Tasks! It is so satisfying to tick off those little boxes as you work your way through your To Do list. Or am I just sad?

A very important goal is to take better care of you! And rewarding yourself is very important along the way to make you want to keep going. Whether it is verbal praise or praise of some other sort, I am sure that you can all think of your own rewards. My reward was (and still is) a cappuccino and a muffin!

I identified myself through my work. Others identify themselves through their relationship or their children. This makes us especially vulnerable to depression if we lose or are forced to give up that one aspect for some reason. I had 'all my eggs in my work basket' and when that went wrong, so did my whole life as my identity was totally wrapped up in my work.

My career had meant everything to me. I had put off having children because of my determination to succeed and provide security for myself and my partner. I felt all the more need to achieve as I had made myself the major breadwinner in our partnership. The more money I earned, the more money we spent. When you earn more, you can always spend it. It became a vicious mental circle that I had to keep going at my unreasonable pace to sustain our standard of living. I was terrified of losing what we had. The more we did have, the more terrified I became of losing it. I was fuelling my own fear.

These have been my experiences but having spoken to many fellow sufferers these are some other things that have caused their depression.

Rejection can trigger feelings of depression. No one likes to be or feel rejected.

Feelings of anger can cause depression. It could be anger towards other people or oneself. If you are holding anger in or blocking anger because you are afraid to express yourself or don't know how to express yourself or are not allowed to express yourself, it builds up and becomes weighty and oppressive depression or explosive and destructive rage.

Anger is a difficult emotion for everyone, even those who show it. It is best treated as soon as possible before it gets out of control.

A feeling of powerlessness is another cause of depression. No one likes to feel that they have no control of things that happen to them. Feeling out of control brings frustration and often aggression and hostility. When those forces are turned inward, the result is often depression.

We are all different and all have our own 'story' but the pattern is the same. While it's not nice to feel negative emotions and we don't like feeling them, they are emotions that we are used to and like all bad habits we can always find our way back to them.

British culture is designed around modesty. We are not encouraged to shout about our achievements. Consequently we can end up focusing on the negative. Great when you are suffering from depression!

Have you noticed how some people, or you yourself, feel embarrassed or awkward about telling someone that you're feeling great or that you've had a promotion at work or done very well financially in case they are envious or jealous or you might upset them in some way?

Wouldn't it be nice if we could spread a little of our happiness by calling others when we are happy instead of just calling to moan or be at the receiving end of such a call? That would make me happy to hear someone I care about sounding happy.

For some, the basis of their depression remains a mystery. I feel that it helps to find out the cause as you can only start dealing with it if you know what it is. I believe that if we are unable to figure out 'why' it keeps us stuck in depression.

Some people disagree with me. They argue if you figure out why you are depressed and think you cannot do anything to change the situation, it might make the situation worse. If you can ask why, objectively, then I believe it can only help to find out why.

Have you ever thought, 'Why me?' If you have, I would like to bet that the answer you came up with wasn't very helpful to you. This type of question and thinking is very negative and can be destructive and dangerous if done without guidance from your doctor or counsellor or therapist who can teach you how to replace such negative questions with better ones, as it usually results in a punishing downward spiral of a never ending answer.

Knowing the cause is not enough to produce a solution but it is a start. I had to learn what to do to change, how to do it, when to do it and how to sustain it and enjoy it. I found lots of people out there to show me how to do that.

I am sure that if we all had time to just step back and examine our lives with a panel of experts made up of, let's say, a life coach, a medical expert and a nutritionist and a psychologist, most of us would be horrified. We laugh at the observational humour of comedians who make fun of our lives but should we be laughing or taking mental notes?

The list for the causes of depression can be endless. I'm sure you can think of many more.

Maybe the cause of your Depression is different again. Maybe you would like to share it with others on my website: www.depressioncanbefun.com.

I believe strongly that something causes depression and the depression is the body and mind shutting down to protect itself and to give itself the time to heal. Your body and mind take on that maternal role: 'If you're not going to help yourself I'll do it for you'.

Depression often comes at the end of a very long mental or physical fight and unhappy time when the person seems to be, thinks, or tries to convince themselves that they are coping but really they are not.

I couldn't see the seriousness of my own situation or what it was taking out of me as I was too wrapped up in being "down" and fighting on. I needed help to find out what had led me to this state of depression and needed help to lift me out of it and discover happiness again.

It is important that you understand how serious depression is. In most cases, it has not occurred suddenly. It may seem like it has to you. You may feel you were alright until last week, last month or last year and that this has happened all of a sudden.

The last precipitating event may have been an accumulation of stresses in your life, but this is just the last straw to break the camel's back as it were.

If you had been OK, these factors would not have triggered depression.

Your current state is a consequence of things you have done in the past too. The recent past is important but the distant past is also important.

I was 30 when my Depression became too much for me to bear and I tried to kill myself and now I am 40. That's a long time. I don't want the same thing to happen to you.

You may think at the moment that you do not want to get better. Only you can decide if and when. I prefer when!!

AND WHAT ARE THE SYMPTOMS ANYWAY?

I don't like to talk about symptoms and indeed have even stopped myself from reading side-effects and symptoms of the various drugs I've been prescribed over the years for fear of suffering the 'psychological symptoms'. Let's face it, depression brings enough problems of its own without imagining any more.

Having said that, I want to mention them anyway even if it is just to show that you're not alone if you are feeling, have felt or are showing any of these symptoms.

Depression rarely spared me the painful accompanying symptoms of feeling guilt, anger, powerlessness, failure, grief, low self-esteem, insecurity, frustration, conflict with myself and others, anxiety, paranoia and rejection. I did not like who I'd become at all. I felt like a completely different person. I felt like I had lost the real me. I could hardly believe what was happening to me and who I had become.

Helplessness and low self-esteem pretty much sum up the toxic core of depression. Dysfunctional feelings and distorted thinking move in and take over.

Do you suffer from stress? Do you feel overtired and overwhelmed by what you have to do and unable to cope?

Are you sleeping all the time but still waking up exhausted? Or do you toss and turn at night and struggle to get to sleep? Are you having nightmares?

Depression Can Be Fun

Do you feel anxious, irritable, overloaded? Do you feel restlessness or spaciness, a sense of detachment or withdrawal from others? Do you feel burdened or weighed down? Are you starting to feel older? Are you unable to think logically any more? Does every situation seem like a trauma?

If so, you could be suffering from depression. This is how I felt and I was suffering from depression. If you feel this way you probably are too. These are all common symptoms of depression.

Like me you probably also feel guilty for being depressed when so many people depend on you, and scold and punish yourself for failing to live up to your own high expectations. This guilt and self-blame only drags you down even further.

It's not your fault. Your guilt isn't helping anyone. You are punishing yourself which is another symptom of depression. When you do something wrong (in your eyes!) you are likely to punish yourself in an excessive way by scolding yourself and calling yourself names and even with self-destructive behaviour and habits such as binge eating or excessive drinking or self-harm.

When I thought that I had not performed at work or at home, I used to thump myself really hard or hit my head against the wall until it really hurt. Whatever I did, it had to really hurt. No one else was disappointed in me or my performance but I would make it my job to literally beat myself up. I believed that I needed to be punished.

As a trader for a large investment bank in the City of London, I went from being able to read the Financial Times every morning on the tube on the way to work cover to cover in 20 minutes, to not being able to read an article in a weekly magazine without having to re-read the first four lines over and over again. It's really frightening, frustrating and 'depressing' what happens to your mind and body when you are suffering from depression.

I used to frustrate myself no end by the fact that I STILL couldn't do this or that. "I still can't drag myself out of bed in the morning". The word 'still' used to have a very different meaning for me. I used to be able to jump out of bed at 4 am, keep going at work until 10 or 11 pm and still go to the gym before going home to bed and I still managed to have a great social life". "Why can't I do any of it anymore?" "Why can't I achieve anything in a day?" I couldn't even achieve a simple goal I set myself of doing the ironing in a day. I used to become hysterical with frustration and anguish at not achieving anything, not doing anything.

Efforts by my husband to console me were thwarted by my violent thrashing of arms and legs and screaming but it didn't stop him from trying again and again. Most of the time I would sob into my pillow distraught, or rock back and forth in my seat or rub my legs repeatedly and think that nothing mattered in my life any more; I had lost everything and everyone that mattered. I lost my job and with that all my qualifications that I had worked so hard for, my career, my life and friends in the City, all my income, my dignity and pride. I'D LOST ME. My life was just nothingness. I enjoyed nothing, loved nothing, did nothing and achieved nothing.

Other symptoms include feelings of worthlessness, inadequacy, isolation and despair – and along with that, you believe that no one understands or sympathises with you.

Depression can cause a major loss of self-esteem, more so than any other illness, just because it is so hard to define, recognise and describe.

You feel you have no control over what will happen and presume the worst possible scenario in every situation. So you feel helpless and useless.

Often this goes along with loss of interest in work or home life (often in everything really), inability to concentrate on anything, sluggish thought process and in severe cases delusions, which I also suffered from.

I believed that the whole world was against me and that my company was plotting against me and no one could convince me otherwise.

The mind is a very powerful thing. If it goes wrong, you've got problems.

We need to nurture our minds. It's all very well to say it, I know. The pressure of the world today to pay the mortgage, feed, clothe and educate yourself and the kids, look good, move up the social and economic ladder is never ending.

Irritability is another symptom that often accompanies low mood swings.

Often I withdrew and became preoccupied with focusing all my thoughts and attention on my problems. I became overly and unreasonably demanding and dependent. I had no control over my depressed mood and made no secret of my low feelings.

Thoughts of suicide and death were never far away. When I was not thinking about suicide, I was thinking about death all the time and often didn't hesitate to say so out loud much to the distress and despair of loved ones.

I lost interest in sex or any close contact. Depression is a 'mental illness', but often has as many physical symptoms as mental symptoms. The feelings or emotions that are depressive symptoms actually begin to cause the physical effects.

I experienced many physical symptoms like loss of energy, a feeling of 'heaviness', difficult and/or slow movement, a dry mouth, indigestion, and a combination of constipation, diarrhoea or IBS. I gained weight, other sufferers may lose weight and women may have period problems.

I suffered from Irritable Bowel Syndrome (IBS) for a long time when very stressed at work and when I was depressed but didn't think that it was related to my Depression. We are all experts in our own fields. As I said before you wouldn't expect a plumber to sort out your house insurance, so why would we in this mad world that we live in necessarily realise that our Irritable Bowel Syndrome (IBS) was a symptom of stress. It's often the way the body tells us it's not happy.

I gave up looking after and caring about myself and my body. I did not think that I was worth it. Depression by its very nature is selfish and I became very introvert and self-obsessed.

Severe exaggerated thinking and overreacting took over. Depression totally dimmed and diminished the accuracy of my view of reality. I remember my father coming to stay with us in Hampshire. He cut his finger on a small knife and it bled (as it would!). I became hysterical. I thought he was going to die. All I could think was that I was going to lose my dad. I was sobbing uncontrollably. My father was horrified by such an extreme reaction and that was the first time he realised that there was something really wrong.

Friends and family might see it before you do. Pretend you are doing one of those questionnaires in a gossip magazine to find out your perfect partner and see how many of these you would put a tick against. There is no simple definition of depression. If you are wondering if you are down or depressed, check all the list of symptoms here. In general, the more symptoms you have from this list, the more likely it is that you have depression. If you are in doubt, talk with a professional or your GP.

I saw myself as helpless and unable to change myself or my situation. Problems seemed more complicated. My thinking became riddled with exaggeration. Irrational conclusions that I came to with such distorted and faulty reasoning just made my Depression and unhappiness worse. I literally wore myself out with all the worrying and thinking, so much so that I couldn't do much to change my situation at that point. I simply had no energy left to do so as I wasted it all on conjuring up all the worst things in the world that could happen. My husband was always saying to me, "That's the depression talking".

I craved energy and adrenalin and as I didn't have any of my own, I sought it by consuming vast amounts of stimulants like tea and coffee. My brother remembers a day he spent with me when I was between Priory incarcerations. I insisted on stopping for four coffees in my favourite coffee shop, interspersed with half hour shopping interludes. It was ridiculous. It was a total obsession and the results were always so short-lived that another fix was never far away.

Before I 'got ill', I considered my body to be that 'temple' that all the health gurus talk about and supped caffeine-free supplements in an attempt to save my body from the 200 or more poisonous components in a cup of coffee that my nutritionist friend keeps reminding me of. I avoided caffeine if I could. Now I couldn't get enough of it. Maybe again, I was punishing my body subconsciously or maybe I am reading too much into it and maybe I just needed it. However, now that I am feeling much better, I do make an effort to limit myself again to a couple of cups of tea and coffee a day. Sure, it's addictive but what else can make your Monday morning meeting bearable – or your Monday morning full-stop actually? At least it's addictive and legal!

OCDS (obsessive compulsive disorders) can be a precursor to the onset of depression or a symptom of depression. Addiction of any kind is a set up or precondition for depression. They certainly were in my case. For a couple of years before my Depression, I had become obsessive about the gym and cleaning my house. As I mentioned earlier, on the surface, this behaviour might appear to be admirable. You could say that sounds great, but if behaviour is becoming obsessive, it could be a way of avoiding confronting difficult feelings.

My sister said that my 14 hour days, the gym and my hours of obsessive bleaching everything in sight, left no time to talk to me. She felt that she lost me as a sister and a friend long before I was officially diagnosed as 'ill'.

When she used to come to stay with me in London and would kindly have dinner ready for me on my return home from work, I would be more concerned with the untidy kitchen and would immediately set about cleaning up (even though she had already done so!). I remember a friend of mine cooking a curry for me. I was so upset that my house smelled of curry that I don't even remember thanking her for her kind gesture. In fact I was probably noticeably disturbed and distant.

Personally I think that my sister suffers from OCD but she assures me that there is definitely a difference between being 'anally retentive' (like my sister!), Peter Perfect (like my father) and an OCD (like me!).

Studies have shown that creative people can be more predisposed to depression[9]. Does that mean that I'm creative?

Maybe that's why we were encouraged to paint and draw in the hospital or maybe they were hoping to

---

[9] An interview by an American clinical psychologist, Kay Jamison, (1993) (Touched with fire: Manic depressive illness and the artistic temperament. New York: Free Press) of award winning European writers, poets, painters, sculptors and blues musicians, reported that approximately half had suffered from a major depressive episode and nearly two thirds exhibited recurrent severe mood swing tendencies.

discover us and make even more money out of us over and above the extortionate fees!

A girl with schizophrenia whom I met in the NHS hospital had a real talent for brilliant catchy marketing slogans. She enjoyed making them up and she did it so easily. She was amazing. Marketing companies pay people lots of money for the kind of talent she had.

We all have our talents. It is just a matter of knowing what they are and harnessing them and if we enjoy them too, what are we waiting for? Oh yes, get better first! Use this time to re-evaluate your life, remember what used to give you pleasure when you were growing up, when you had time to enjoy yourself. To kick start yourself back on track what did you used to really enjoy doing as a child? What activity used to give you the most pleasure? Try it and see what you come up with.

I do remember playing schools and teaching my siblings and my next door neighbour's children their times tables when I was about 10. Maybe I should have been a teacher?

Apart from shopping, I can't think of much else that I enjoyed! So that's where my problems started! Why didn't I become a personal shopper? Picking and buying clothes at other peoples' expense would have made my husband a lot happier and maybe quenched my desire for spending money without setting new records in overdraft limits.

My husband has always thought that my compulsive spending was a symptom of depression. I think he was hoping that it would go away with my recovery but I think that shopping and spending is an obsession that most women have and don't actually want a cure for anyway. We just want more money to fund it!

Apparently there is an SSRI antidepressant in the US called Cipramil (citalopram) which helps this 'shopaholism' that could help us women 'suffering' from this habit. Let's hope it never reaches our shores ladies!

My husband asked my doctor about it. I couldn't tell you if it works as I managed to escape that particular drug!

I went to one of many motivational seminars where the speaker was talking about self-worth. He inferred that if someone looks at a label on a clothing garment and thinks that it is too expensive, s/he actually thinks that s/he is not worth it.

I wish that that rule of thumb had worked for me. The fact that I had no money should have stopped me. I didn't like myself very much but that didn't stop me spending money either. My train of thought was that if I carried on spending money, I could still pretend that my life was OK and that I was still earning my good salary and that I hadn't lost everything. It was denial.

I do know that spending is not listed in the medical journals' definition of clinical depression but it is on the list for bipolar or manic depression and my excessive spending started when my diagnosis changed to bipolar depression. (See appendix for Diagnostic and Statistical Manual of Mental Disorders.[10])

---

[10] See Appendix 1

We often don't know we need help until we wake up one morning and are faced with a problem that seems insurmountable. Anxiety can creep up on us and changes in our life can be so subtle that we don't notice that things have gone badly wrong.

Many of us become such experts at burying uncomfortable or stressful feelings that we fool ourselves into believing that they have disappeared. Nothing could be further from the truth. Often they are emotional time-bombs, ready to explode when we least expect them to.

Admitting to yourself that you need help is the first step in tackling a problem. It is worth familiarising yourself with the above pointers and taking time out occasionally to ask yourself honestly if you need help.

I found keeping a mood diary very useful, not just to record events of the day but also to record how I was feeling throughout the day. I found this helpful in that it helped me monitor my moods and revealed patterns of my mood cycles and situations, feelings and time periods associated with my Depression and now I can spot the warning signs and spring into action with my 'New Pill Regime'.

I also used to find it helpful to write down the three most positive things about my day last thing at night before going to bed (if I made it that far in the day before going to bed that is). Even if they were tiny positives like I had enjoyed a cup of tea, it used to help me feel less agitated and more relaxed before going to sleep.

Looking back over my diary it was easier to sense when my mood used to drop, to track what kinds of feelings seemed to make my Depression worse and to pinpoint what started to change in my behaviour or attitude when a depressive episode was coming on.

This takes time and practice like everything but you can start to detect the signals and warning signs, rather like the warning signs of a migraine, and act immediately. For example, if you notice that your children are causing your Depression to worsen when they are naughty, you can't change them (you already know that as you've tried!) or remove them from your life (other than temporarily locking them in their room!) but you can work on ways to help you to change the way you react to them to keep your mood stable. As much as other peoples' actions may upset us, we have little control over other people and can only change how we react to their actions. I've learned that the hard way as I am sure many of us have. If only we learned by listening to our parents but none of us do, do we? We have to 'get burned' ourselves!

Depression makes you believe in your own negative thinking and your negative thinking makes you hold on to your Depression. It is a vicious cycle you must break.

My thinking was totally text book and I could tick every one of the points below. Read on and see if they apply to you at the moment.

1. All or nothing thinking. Very black and white categories. Anything short of perfect is failure and no good.
2. Overgeneralisation
3. Dwelling on a single negative detail to the point of disillusionment.

4. Disqualifying the positive. Rejecting positive experience as not counting and so maintaining negative bias.
5. Jumping to conclusions. Always negative of course.
    a. Mind reading – thinking someone is reacting negatively to you and will not be convinced otherwise.
    b. Fortune Telling - Anticipating things will turn out badly and feel convinced your prediction is an established fact.
6. Magnification (catastrophising) or minimisation
7. Negative emotional reasoning
8. Should – Trying to motivate oneself with should and should not and must/ought to.
9. Labelling and mislabelling – Negative labels, 'I'm a failure'
10. Personalisation – self blame for external events that one is not responsible for.

These are all the kinds of errors in thinking that depression produces. Remember that they are symptoms of depression and not in any way a character failing. Fortunately, they are fairly consistent among individuals and are therefore easily diagnosed and can be very successfully treated through therapy (see chapters on Therapy). You shouldn't expect to handle these difficult feelings and symptoms yourself. There is help out there.

You will be able to solve the problems (even if they seem insurmountable now), you will cope with stressful events better and feel much better about yourself, and you will feel your spirits lift.

The mind is a very powerful tool. Use it wisely, it needs regular maintenance.

Come on everyone, let's do it, let's get better, TOGETHER!

"WORK HAS A LOT TO ANSWER FOR"

Work to live NOT live to work.

Blood's not good enough these days is it? They're not happy until they've got wind of your divorce or separation because what does that mean for them? It means that we throw ourselves into our work of course to forget how bad our home life is, even though it's our bloody work life that forced our private life to collapse in the first place and indeed will keep it there as there'll be no time now to build a new one!

100% is not enough. People give 150% or are expected to. It is not achievable because it is not possible; in maths or life.

84% of depression is work related but the fear of derailing our careers in this dog eat dog world is enough to stop us from asking for help at work and the problem is self-perpetuating.

We've all heard of YUPPIES (Young Upwardly Mobile Professional), DINKIES (Double Income No Kids) and what's the latest nickname? Oh yes, LATs (Living Apart Together). People are getting married but carry on living on their own in separate houses with their own lives. It's the modern day attempt to be together. Work commitments keep people living apart but we are actually all scared of being alone so we invest in a future husband or wife for when we retire! It's the closest we're going to get until we retire and we want to make sure that the best haven't all been taken so we take one now! Has the world really gone mad or is it me? I used to think it was me and that was part of my problem. Now I think that it's the world and I feel much better.

In the 60s when the world was normal, people took Acid to feel crazy. Now the world is crazy, people take Prozac to feel normal!

Apparently I'm now 'DISCO' woman: I have to say I like the sound of my new label: Discerning, Increasing years, Stylish and Comfortably Off. To qualify for this label, one has to be 'in shape without resorting to girdles and giant brassieres and be financially independent, having worked incredibly hard for well-nigh 20 years'.

That may be, but I don't feel like Disco woman right now!

We all do so much and try to squeeze so much into our day.

Can you relate to having to pinch loo roll from your office because by the time you've finished your 17 hour day, even the 24 hour stores have closed? Well you know what I mean. It's even that God awful cheap stuff that you wouldn't be seen dead buying in the supermarket even if you were on the bread line. We're working harder than ever and don't even get the basic luxury of plush toilet roll because we don't have the time to go and get it.

Thank goodness for the internet supermarket but I've always been useless with weights and sizes and measurements and still find myself with family sized bags of potatoes and children's party sized cartons of orange juice and enough bacon to feed the Street. Still at least I eat!

I worked in the city as a trader on the trading floor for two major investment houses for many years. It involved long hours, lots of studying for trading exams, working with some fabulous and very stimulating, fun, intelligent people, lots of heated temperaments, stress, fast decisions, studying and knowing the market, trusting your instinct, weighing up situations, studying the charts, anticipating market reactions, waiting for breaking news, interpreting company figures and Fed decisions on interest rates and payroll numbers, early morning meetings to discuss the day's news, strategy meetings, profit and loss accounting, not moving from your desk or your computer screen all day, good financial rewards for success and hard work, lots of travel, lots of reading and learning and lots of excitement, failure, disappointments, frustration, success, reward, lots of client entertainment, late nights and early mornings.

It was hard work but great fun and still very much a man's world. I felt very proud, lucky and honoured to have been a part of it.

It was a career that just developed really. I didn't plan it. I had hoped to have children one day but I ended up being the major bread winner and wrapped up in the quest for doing more, working harder, earning more, spending more and not much time for much else.

In my mind, I couldn't stop and have children as I wouldn't be able to afford to stay at home and care for them given that my husband was self-employed, away at a moment's notice for long periods of time with no guaranteed, regular income.

I was scared of giving up our security and in an effort to increase our security by taking a new job that offered me more money, I hastened the inevitable crash. I made a huge mistake by changing my amazing job in a Company where I felt honoured and proud, to a role in a very different Company with very different people where I was considered to be 'superhuman' for coming from my old firm which really is the The Best there is. Within six months the workload and lack of support became too much and I collapsed. I was extremely ill with mental and physical exhaustion, depression and feeling suicidal and totally incapable of any type of work.

These were probably the years in which my husband and I would have sensibly tried for children while I was in my thirties. I did ask my husband and my doctors a few times about children during my illness as they were very much on my mind but they advised against it given my Depression and the medication that I was taking.

As I was getting better, I asked my husband about children but he said that he felt that he was too old and now that I am much better, our marriage has fallen apart and it's too late.

I do feel sad for my husband as he would have made a great dad and I feel that I have denied him that opportunity but I feel sad for me too as I would have loved a family. No one chooses to be ill and I feel that we have missed out on so much together.

What's it all about? It's ridiculous.

At least quite a few of us are beginning to ask ourselves that question. That's of course if you're sensible and can still see clearly enough and rationalise to make that decision to get out before it's made for you by, in my case and in the case of many, a breakdown and years of serious clinical depression and a separation after a very happy 14 year relationship to a very special man; or more seriously a stroke; heart attack; panic attacks; the list is endless.

I was out with my mother-in-law at the ballet when she introduced me to a friend of hers who used to be a banker. At 45 he had a stroke and is in a wheelchair paralysed and unable to speak. Unfortunately you cannot swap wealth for health. It's worth thinking about folks.

WHEN THE SHIT HITS THE FAN

You never know whats round the corner.....

What would you do if you lost your career, lost your marbles, then lost your husband and your friends? Thank goodness the latter was only temporary. Well here's what not to do!

As I lie here in bed thinking “Same shit, different day”, the phone rings. It's my dad again with his ‘reassuring’ line “Don't worry darling, you never know what's round the corner!” Yeh, right! We've all been round lots of corners and none have ever come up with the goods yet.

Maybe I don't want to know what's around the next corner and am quite happy hiding behind this one where nothing else can get at me and hurt me even more. What if it gets worse? So why did I go and see another psychic yesterday? I guess I'll keep going until one tells me what I want to hear; that everything is going to be OK, that I'll be healthy, wealthy, and happy.

I used to be so positive and level headed and independent. Sound familiar! You're supposed to get more self-assured and happier as you get older. That's what they tell you. That's just to make you feel better about getting old, grey and wrinkled I'm sure. Maybe they tell you that to keep you at the grindstone with the carrot dangling just always around that flipping corner! So what happened?

My difficult childhood obviously had something to do with it but it didn't feel like it at the time. Yes I had a difficult childhood, with very fiery parents always at each other's throats (though very much in love) and my mother's suicide, but I felt like I was a pretty well balanced child and now adult. I saw it as character building. This never came up as an issue in my therapy. Lots of people have difficult childhoods. Lots of parents fight. My mother died tragically but it is nature's way that parents die before their children. Yes she died much earlier than we would all have liked but some children are unfortunate to lose their parents even earlier than I did.

Maybe 10 years in the city did it to me, but that was work hard, play hard and I thoroughly enjoyed the buzz and my lifestyle.

Could it have been my relationship and marriage? I don't think so. I was very happy with my Scottish 'Indiana Duncs' as my friends used to call him!

I basically worked myself into the ground; despite the warning signs; despite everyone telling me to stop; despite feeling extremely stressed out and tearful and even suicidal.

This wasn't enough to make me stop. One day I just snapped and tried to kill myself.

It wasn't until there was a mistake at work and I became the scapegoat, that I stopped. It wasn't me that stopped even then. The situation was taken out of my hands and I was suspended from work pending an investigation.

I was reinstated a few days later when the investigation had taken place but in my highly sensitive state, the damage had already been done. In my eyes, everything I had worked for and studied for had been taken away in a moment and my honour and loyalty were in question and I had been stripped of my dignity. Something just snapped inside my already fractious, exhausted head and I tried to kill myself.

I would have been spared any publicity as I was immediately reinstated and the whole situation would have blown over as mistakes happen every day in any job. I brought the publicity on myself with 'a suicide attempt' and a rather long stay in the Roehampton Priory. Well you would really wouldn't you? I always was a bit of a drama queen but this was a bit extreme and I really had no control over my actions.

My poor husband had just flown up to Scotland the day that I tried to kill myself. He found out when he landed in Scotland and had to turn around and come right back again.

The huge court case that followed that was covered very publicly by the national press didn't help matters much either.

I wouldn't recommend letting it get to the stage that I did before seeking help. Don't let it become a bigger problem that it has to be and make sure you take your life back before 'the shit hits the fan'. Take your life back before depression takes your life away from you. You would make sure that your best friend got help. Treat yourself like your best friend. You owe it to yourself. If you can't do it for yourself, do it for someone you love or who loves you. Be kind to yourself.

THE ROOT OF ALL EVIL ...MONEY!

Money! Yep, I think that's it. Can't live with it, can't live without it! That too sounds familiar doesn't it!

I'm sticking to Lulu Guinness's suggestion from now on; you can be too rich or too thin.

Can I give you a piece of that advice I was talking about?

When you are happy and someone comes along and offers you less work, more fun and three times your salary, don't do it! In fact, don't believe it! It's the devil in disguise. I fell for it. Not easily, I may say in self-defence, but that really doesn't make any difference as I did succumb and years later I'm still paying the price and you know what else: If one more person says to me that everything happens for a reason and even worse, that I will be a better person for it, I will seriously have to... strongly disagree.

How can having a nervous breakdown, subsequent depression for years, worrying all my family, friends and husband, who spent the first years of our married life locking all the doors and windows every night and watching me 24/7 in case I got out and killed myself, no sex ever since your wedding night with your husband and gaining four stones in weight have a reason?

'What doesn't kill you makes you stronger', was obviously a quote from an insane person.

There is that song written about money and how it makes the world go round. I know from experience and what I've seen others experience that a lack of it can make you depressed. Unfortunately, my world was out of control, and so was my spending. Not that I cared at the time.

I was having a hard time and no, it is not an excuse, my psychiatrist said so! When I think about my spending, it really upsets me. I spent so much on so many things I didn't really need.

I spent so much time with personal shoppers who made me feel wonderful – I do recommend them really, as they are free and know what they are doing, unlike me, who went a little mad from time to time. Time to time, who am I kidding! Well to be honest, I kidded myself for a long time and still do, when I need a fix, and we all need a fix from time to time. The difference is back then, from time to time, meant from morning till night.

I needed to feel good and shopping did that, OK it was only temporary, but that buzz made me feel valued, feel powerful almost, feel worthy. The cost, the bills; I didn't really think about how much I was spending, we'd worked hard, we could afford it, couldn't we? I couldn't think about whether we could afford it, I needed something and I needed it now, couldn't my husband see that? He could see the goods I brought home, he could see the bills, he could see our vanishing account, but I was blind, all I could see was how black and empty my life felt and I needed to fill the void quickly and painlessly and NOW.

I took retail therapy to the extreme though and didn't just spend money on myself. I just spent money! One day my husband had just got back from a business trip abroad when he got a call from his brother who was doing some work at our house, to say that a truck of antique furniture had arrived at the house and that the drivers had unloaded the van and vanished so quickly that he feared I may have paid over the odds for them. My poor husband admitted to me recently that he just wanted to get back on the plane and go back to where he had just come from. He just could not handle any more.

Not long before that he had tried to get us out of a purchase of three very expensive paintings that I had made at yet another art exhibition in Edinburgh by telling them that I was mentally ill! The gallery agreed that if anyone else wanted to buy the paintings, then I would not have to buy them. Funnily enough no one else did so we ended up with three very expensive paintings which still hang on our walls today as we can't sell them!

We ended up with quite a few other pieces of art in very much the same way which make my husband feel quite nauseous when he looks at them due to the amount of money they cost that we didn't have. I wasn't even in to art but that didn't seem to matter to me. It was just the act of spending money that I was addicted to.

So I spent and spent. I loved the feeling of being in control. Why have one, when I could have the set? Why have one colour, when I could have several to match different outfits? I needed to be prepared. I don't know why, because I could never face going to parties and I wasn't well enough to go back to work. But I bought just in case!

I felt so unimportant and desperately wanted to feel important and loved feeling important (don't we all?), so going into really expensive shops was a real buzz. I stopped looking at the price tags, they were irrelevant and I didn't want to be reminded of how much I was spending anyway. In the expensive shops you get more compliments when you try on the stuff and I tried on lots and bought lots.

It didn't stop at clothes either. I bought food, coffee, sunglasses, and furniture. Surprisingly I never bought holidays; the one thing that would have benefited me and my husband totally was something that never entered my head to buy, maybe because I would have had to wait to enjoy what I had bought and I wanted my fix 'now'. I know my sister paid for us to go to a Health Farm and I enjoyed that and gladly bought the products used in my treatments, believing they would make me feel a million dollars as I had been promised.

Every shopping trip, I always made time for a coffee with friends or just a coffee on my own, with a muffin one day and a panini the next, generally accompanied by a magazine. The coffee shop was my well earned break, my time to look over my shopping, proud of what

I had bought. It provided breathing space before I started my next trip somewhere; it was my safe haven, and a luxury that became the norm. I found pleasure in drinking cappuccino, another addictive substance, not that I knew it at the time. As far as I was concerned, it complemented my lifestyle, the lifestyle I had always wanted and could not possibly afford.

My sister is very good with money, she gets a real buzz saving for an item and then buying it with cash. But I don't deal in cash, in fact I am literally allergic to cash, well nickel anyway, which I use as my excuse for using credit cards!

Anyway, my sister saved for a year to buy a blender (cost £69.99) and OK, by the time that she had saved enough to buy it, it had been reduced to half the price, but that is because by then it was dated. Liz didn't mind, she got a real buzz from having saved the money and then only having to pay £35.00 which meant she could buy something else or in her case, save more quickly for something else.

I bought the same device at the time it was full price and let her admire it for free. I got a buzz because I bought it there and then. OK, that buzz lasted for as long as it took to pay for it on my credit card, take it home, open the box, wrestle with the packaging and put it on my side. Then the novelty wore off and I realised it didn't go with anything else in the kitchen – so back to the shop I went to buy other kitchen gadgets that did match. And so the buzz kept me going.

The odd £25 here and there adds up to £100s very quickly and too easily. My husband advised me to write everything down I spent in a day. He even bought me a little book for that purpose. The truth is that I didn't want to know. The few times I did write everything down I was horrified and shocked at how much I was spending every day which probably explains why I didn't do it often enough and why I was in the financial mess I was in.

My credit card took a real bashing when I was depressed, I thought it would make me feel better – retail therapy – there is a lot to be said for that. Unfortunately there is not a lot to be said about the guilt afterwards and the slow realisation that I didn't have a clue how I was ever going to pay it back, or in my case, where I would get more credit from!

A lot of us do it, we spend to feel good, to look great, to treat ourselves, but do we regularly ask if we can afford it or do we simply say "I deserve this". Women and men alike can all spend money they don't possess, but there are different kinds of spenders. Here's my view of the types. Do you recognise yourself as any of these?:

There are the "Guilty Spenders": the ones that spend on themselves, then feel guilty so spend on their partners or loved ones to make themselves feel better.

There are the "Needy Spenders", who justify their need for all those shoes, and clothes to make themselves feel good.

There are the "You Spenders", who spend money making themselves look adorable, having botox, cosmetic surgery, having their hair done, so that you will find them more attractive; it is just for you. Be thankful I am not letting myself go!

There are the "Must Have it Spenders", who would kill for certain items because they cannot live without them, it says so on the advert or they are the latest fashions. I was that woman insisting on trying trousers in the Liz Hurley style of that safety pin dress that I looked ridiculous in. I couldn't see the mutton dressed as lamb. Thank goodness for my friends providing me with a reality check.

There are the "Emotional Spenders", who spend to make themselves feel better. They buy this and that, because they need the comfort. They need to feel wonderful and shopping makes them feel wonderful. Getting the bill doesn't, but that is at least a month away. When they get the bill, they need to go shopping again, because they are depressed again and need cheering up.

There are the "Impulsive Spenders", who spend literally on impulse. They see it and have to have it. They will die if they don't get it now. Now, meaning this second without pausing to think about it.

There are the "Worrying Spenders", who spend the same as the rest of us, but worry more about whether this will go with that and how much they have spent and how they will pay for all those items, and how they will get it all in the car. They do not think that to stop themselves worrying they should stop spending.

There are the "Pessimistic Spenders", who spend because they might not be here tomorrow to enjoy shopping or spending the money they have earned. They are the shoppers who complain about spending, how much things cost but then buy it anyway. They may look miserable and moan but don't be fooled they secretly love shopping just like the rest of us.

Of course, you have the "Optimistic Shoppers" too, the ones who smile whilst knowing that they have just exceeded their credit card limit. These are people who squeeze themselves into a dress size smaller than they are used to, just to get the discount or the satisfaction when they tell their friends how small they are.

There are the "Gadget Spenders", who justify spending all that money because a certain gadget is going to save them time. Time they need to go shopping! You know the gadget that takes you an earth to get out of the packaging and then you never use.

There are the "Deserving Spenders", I earn it, so I can spend it, above and beyond my means, I work hard, so I deserve a treat now and again; sorry did I say now and again, silly me, I deserve it all the time.

There are the "Future Spenders", "well I bought it because you never know when I might need it". Ok, they have never worn it, but if they were ever a size 6, it would be perfect. It will be perfect when they lose weight, it will go perfectly with all the other clothes in the spare bedroom they bought for the same reason.

There are the "Parent Shoppers", who spend a whole load of money on their kids. They have to have those special trainers they never had when they were children. They can be the most aggressive because they don't care what it takes; their child will die without them or the shame of not having them (well the parents will anyway!) when their neighbour's child has!

There is the "Secret Shopper", who buys exactly what they want and then hides yet another pair of expensive shoes in the cupboard, ashamed of what they have spent. They know they can't afford them but at some point, when they feel less guilty, they will bring them out and when asked are they new and how much they cost, they respond "Oh these old things, I've had them for ages!"

There are the "Bargain Spenders", who buy something because it is a bargain, and they would be a fool to let that get away. They don't need it but it was on offer, they got a bargain!

There are the "Show Off Spenders", the ones that buy it to make others take note. They love to say where they got it and how much it cost. They actually get more from your reaction than actually buying the item.

There are the "Addictive Spenders", who buy the same stuff over and over again, as this particular item gives them a buzz like no other. The cupboards can be full of jars of coffee but they keep buying more. They don't think about it, they just keep buying more.

Then you have the "Safe Spenders". I wish I could be one of these. They budget well and save for the something and then buy it. Alas, there is only a very small percentage of this group of spenders in the 21st Century, the rest of us just buy on credit whether we have the money or not.

You could be any of these but if you're like me you could be all of them (except for the safe spender of course!) What happened to shopping for necessity!? My husband says my illness put a stop to that.

This is not just a female pastime. It affects us all.

Supermarkets, my God, I spend so much on food these days, because I want to eat better. Now I can buy organic food too (organic means I can buy incredibly expensive healthy vegetables). Yes I can upgrade my vegetables from healthy to healthy organic by just buying carrots that tell me they are organic, but are they really with all that packaging and all those Air Miles?

I tried to go up the medicine aisle. Less temptation you might think; think again. At the top of that aisle is make-up (they believe that even if you are ill, you still want and feel you need to look your best), so I got milk, make up and paracetamol, but I can only buy 16 paracetamol (one packet) in one shop. Apparently Government policy, so feeling controlled I bought two packets of Lemsip, three packets of throat sweets, some cough medicine and four boxes of plasters – they were on special offer: buy three get one free, just to feel liberated from the Government legislation – no one tells me what I can spend my money on, in this case, my credit card purchases are my call.

Some supermarkets are open 24 hours a day, but if you miss their opening hours, you can always shop on-line!

Ahh the internet, you can shop from your own home with your credit card, from anywhere in the world. You are not restricted to your own town or your own country. You can buy cheap/expensive things/gadgets/devices from all over the world. You can download the latest annoying mobile ring tones for a small fee from your computer, you can even get a man on line, and you can order all these devices to be delivered to your home (when you are not in because you are out shopping.)

That is, except the man obviously, you cannot have him delivered yet, you still have to meet him, you can look and vet before you purchase though, sorry did I say purchase, I meant meet – shopping on the brain!

So you have the delivery card posted to say you were out when they tried to deliver. You couldn't even be bothered to wait in for the express delivery you ordered. You can't remember what it is, it was not the only thing you ordered in the early hours of the morning, but you were sure you needed it and couldn't do without it. It was advertised everywhere, so you had to get one, everyone else has one and you don't want to be the only one without one, whatever it is!

Thinking about that has really depressed me. Now I need a cappuccino to make me feel better, where are the car keys? I could use my new gadgety thing that makes the perfect cappuccino that I bought to save me spending money at the coffee shop in town, but I have not quite read all the instructions. It is plugged in and looks fantastic and I clean it regularly but I cannot be bothered to wait for it. So I will drive the 10 minutes into town (I could walk but I need to pick up some other bits and pieces), buy a £1.00 parking ticket and go to the expensive coffee shop in town, where they know me well enough to know exactly what I want and I can enjoy my new book that I have just purchased and while I am out I can go shopping - food shopping - I have run out of milk. By now you all know that means that I will come home with a lot more than milk which is the reason I need to take the car into town rather than walk. Anyway I am paying gym membership, if I want exercise I can go there.

That brings me to the Gym. Yes I joined a gym, not in January like everyone else. I did it because I wanted to. I get more out of doing something when I want to rather than feeling that I should. I got roped into a six month contract and I convinced myself I would go. Of course I didn't so that's £60 a month until my contract runs out. We've all been there and we all know that's how the gyms make their money.

What is fascinating is that everyone has the shopping bug in some way or form; how serious it is, depends on your state of mind. My mind was pretty crap for seven years, so you can understand how worried my bank manager was! My dad worries but I tell him I still follow his £1.00 theory that: 'Happiness is having £1 and spending 90p. Unhappiness is having £1 and spending £1.10'. I don't think he believes me.

Money gives us options and choices - who am I kidding, it gives me a buzz. My sister says it only gives me a short buzz and that life can give you a bigger buzz if you let it. She believes the shopping buzz has a short shelf life, just like the yellow sticker aisle and she doesn't want to live life on the yellow sticker aisle. She believes that we need to "change our attitude and get gratitude". Being grateful lifts our spirits, a great help in the fight against depression.

Now I wonder where I can buy gratitude, there was a deal on at that shop on the corner "three for two, get cheapest free". Now, where did I put my keys!?

THE HUSBAND

Poor guy. My husband really drew the short straw. He waited until 40 to find 'The Right One' and as soon as he married me, I became someone else and certainly not the person he had met and fallen in love with some eight years earlier. He fell in love with a NORMAL, fun loving, positive, athletic, energetic, determined, busy, intelligent, city trader. I turned in to a depressed, unconfident, lethargic, overweight sloth. His 'cliff edge proposal' was just the start!

I'm surprised he even made it through our Wedding Day as I was already cracking then as I had started my new job some six months earlier and I ended up telling the man of my dreams to fuck off over something totally unimportant thing like stepping on my toes for the first waltz on what was supposed to be the happiest day of our lives. Well things just went from bad to worse from then on really.

I used to love parties like any young woman and love dancing and socialising but I was already beginning to withdraw and didn't like to be the centre of attention any more. I didn't notice this at the time, but my husband and close friends had.

I had told my husband before the Wedding not to make me do the first Dance but being in high spirits, which you would hope of the Groom on his Wedding Day, he dragged me from my family corner onto the Floor. It was all too much and out came those dreadful words "Fuck off!" He told me that I had ruined his Wedding Day. The next five years didn't get any better. He is a big socialite too and would arrange to meet people and I would try to psyche myself up to go, but at the last minute wouldn't be able to do it.

At first he thought that I was doing it on purpose and that I had no intention of keeping our social engagements, but he made a huge effort to try to understand. This was an extremely frustrating time for him and he spent many lonely nights downstairs watching the television or reading the many books he had scoured the internet for on Understanding Depression and Depression Fallout, which is what they call what the loved ones around the depressed person suffer from as a result of being with, dealing with and caring for a depressed person.

My diagnosed Bipolar Depression manifested itself sometimes in hysteria and sometimes in complete despair. The hysteria was always evident to my husband by my serious shopping sprees on anything and everything and partying non-stop and getting into all sorts of trouble and not sleeping at all for days. He used to live in fear of my manic episodes. The despair was not unlike my days of clinical depression as I would take to my bed for days and weeks on end.

Actually if I had to make a choice, I preferred the bipolar depression as at least I had the high when I was experiencing the manic side of the bipolar depression. I guess I got to do what some people would describe as outrageous/extravagant/exciting things when I was experiencing the mania. It wasn't much of a choice for my husband though as I was either spending the mortgage and worrying him silly or wailing with mental torture into my pillow. Even the 100% goose and down feather pillow, bought at considerable expense on one of my shopping sprees, couldn't drown my wailing. Nothing could drown it.

My husband often tried to reassure me that my negative thinking was 'The Black Dog' taking over and not to believe it. Even now when I find negative thoughts creeping into my head, I automatically think of his voice saying, "That's the Depression talking", or "That's The Black Dog talking" and it helps.

My husband blamed my company for my Depression and for a long time we were involved in a long drawn out legal battle with them which culminated in a groundbreaking court case at the High Court in London. It created lots of publicity and was in all the papers and cost us many thousands of pounds and four years of worry and angst. More importantly it stopped us from getting on with our lives for too long.

Surprising really and honourable that he only threw in the towel in 2006 after seven years of illness. That's when he threw back at me that I had never been a proper wife: That I never picked him up from the airport or cooked for him. That was because I was always working. Actually I did cook but only once I was ill and no longer working. I used to make chocolate cake and lots of it when I was ill. OK, so I ate most of it myself, but he knew where the cake tin was! Where did that four stone come from and so quickly?

I'm devastated of course, but then I'm on the mend finally and in the land of the living again (largely thanks to him) after having spent years on 'happy pills', which did not make me very happy I can tell you, but my husband and my psychiatrist obviously strongly disagree with me on this. I respect my husband's decision as I love him dearly and always will and I want him to be the happy man he used to be.

I misinterpreted his actions for a long time. I thought that he was keeping my friends and family away from me. He was actually trying to protect me. Only he ever saw how I would come back from seeing friends, exhausted, drained and how I would misinterpret what people said to me, how terribly guilty I would feel when anyone did anything for me or went out of their way to come and see me, the effort of pretending to put on an act to be calm and composed in their company. I didn't think that I was worth anyone's time and didn't actually want it. I just wanted to be on my own. He even upset a couple of my friends by being overprotective which they too misinterpreted as keeping them away from me.

He was in a very distressing situation himself as the person he loved had given up on living and just wanted to die and used to tell him so every single day. He saw that I was worse when I saw people as the stress of putting on my act became harder and harder. My care was all down to him and he was doing what he thought was best. A lot of people didn't realise how ill I was given THE ACT and that only served to increase the view that my husband was a Baddie by keeping people away from me. He was the only one who saw my pain and despair.

I now obviously appreciate that he's only human and not a doctor and did what he thought was best at the time with the help of the doctors. So many years out of anyone's life is one hell of a long time and feels even longer when you're forced to live in such unbearable circumstances.

Every time I was in hospital he would visit me every day twice a day which would take up most of his working day given that I was in hospital in London and we lived in Hampshire which is at least a hour's journey each way, traffic and weather permitting and let's face it in England, traffic and weather never permit, at least not at the same time anyway!

His business obviously suffered as he declined so many jobs to avoid leaving me alone for long periods and he was with me all day when he should have been out there making and maintaining those hard-earned contacts which as we all know don't stay as contacts if you don't keep up your profile and contact. "In sickness and in health" really came into its own. Those words just roll off the tongue in the Wedding Ceremony, but by goodness they're harder to honour in such terrible times as I am sure my husband will vouch for.

I'll always love my husband and I think and hope that in his own way he will always love me (love has many guises and I believe that my husband's affectionate jokes are his guise!) but we've been through so much. Since my illness he saw me as his patient rather than his wife and most certainly rather than his lover. That's pretty tough for any man full stop but we all know that it's a no no to sleep with your patient.

Even when I was getting better, sex still seemed a taboo subject for us and unnatural and strange even thinking about it even though I loved him still so deeply and I still fancied him as much as the day I first met him. More in fact, as our first date didn't go too well. It was a blind date arranged by two of our best friends who were already a couple themselves. He didn't like what I was wearing and told me so. I didn't forgive him until several glasses of wine later! I did find it funny though.

We had a lot of fun before I got ill and I am pleased to say that we have fun with each other now and we can and do laugh about what we've been through. I'll admit that I shed a few tears too but he always shakes me out of it with a light hearted joke. He often refers to the period now as 'Happy Days'!

He has helped a lot with the details of my illness for this book as he kept a record of every detail of my illness.

The guy deserves a medal actually. He did think of getting some therapy himself to cope with what he has been through.

Not only was he coping with my Depression; I had severe mood swings, I was violent, deceitful, introverted and very overweight. He read so much on how to cope with depression and with someone who is depressed. He also sent books to my close family and friends to help them understand what I was going through and why I had cut them off and never got in touch.

I do hope that one day I will be able to make it up to my husband for what I have put him through, but how do you give back a person seven years of his or her life?

DEPRESSION FALLOUT

What my family went through doesn't bear thinking about. It's such a cruel illness for everyone concerned. They were despairing. My father lost lots of weight worrying about me. My dad just couldn't believe that his golden girl, who had always been so happy and so successful, was wasting her life in bed and always crying down the phone to him.

My little brother lived on the other side of the world. I say little. He's actually six foot tall and seven years younger than me but he'll always be my little brother. I can't imagine how he must have felt when he used to call and find me distraught at the other end of the phone, screaming most of the time with despair.

I had tried to be like a mother to him since our mother died and when I think and hear him talk now about how he thought I was going to die the same way as his mum, I want to cry. So yes it is selfish and I was selfish but no way would I ever want to hurt these people in my life, who mean so much to me yet I did for years because I wasn't well. I wanted to stop it for them as well.

A lot of people don't understand this. It is an illness. Just because you can't see it, people find it hard to accept it as an illness.

My friends, family and husband found it hard to understand and why should they? They have been fortunate enough not to have suffered from depression themselves. Unless you have been through it how can anyone possibly understand.

Can anyone understand you like another depressive can? Then again you don't really care about anyone because you feel like no one can really appreciate how you feel, because if you don't like yourself, who else can?

- You can be in a room full of people and still feel isolated.
- You can be in a loving relationship and still feel unloved.
- You can be among your closest friends and still feel alone.

It's not just that Monday morning feeling we are talking about here. We have all been there and we all have our down days, crap weeks, months or years when things just don't go right. Sometimes we will look back on New Year's Eve (which let's face it for most of us can be a bit of an anticlimax anyway!) and reflect on how disappointing the last year has been, this is not the depression that I am talking about.

This depression is so desolate, so draining, so all-encompassing that death seems like the only way. I say way. Way to what you may ask? Well a depressive can't even think that far ahead. We're usually so doped up and numbed by this stage we can't even think. It's not an easy way out. After all, what's easy about killing yourself? It's not a way to be released to some great life in the sky. We just can't go on.

I couldn't face anyone. I ignored people's phone calls and just left them brief messages on their answering machines when I knew they would be out to let them know that I'd be in touch.

I was embarrassed and ashamed and too depressed to do anything. I put on so much weight simply because all I did was eat and sleep and take my drugs. The drugs piled on my weight too. I didn't do anything in the house. My husband did everything. He used to religiously cook for me and bring three meals a day to me in bed on a tray. I probably would have wasted away rather than expanded if he hadn't been there to shop and cook. If he hadn't, at least then I wouldn't have had to work so hard at losing that four stone! There's gratitude for you! I do not actually know how he did it, how he coped. He looked so tired. It worries me and upsets me that I was the cause but I did not mean to hurt the man I loved, the man I wanted to marry. If I could have avoided hurting him, I would. I think that he knows that.

Unfortunately the brain is probably the only part of the body that is not fully understood even today in the medical world. The surgeon can't just open you up and fix it or inject some serotonin or give you a new brain and job done. Not yet anyway. It's so much more complicated than that.

My husband describes it as "The Ripple Effect". The depressive is at the epicentre of the emotional explosion and the ripples of depression are felt by everyone who is close to them.

Depression Fallout is the name given to what others who are involved with the depressed person suffer from as a result of caring for and being with that person.

A depressed person affects everyone around them negatively with their mood, their attitude, and their actions. Everything is very hard work and very draining. The mentally ill are exhausting.

If you are not careful, your carer can end up with a form of depression themselves almost by osmosis. It is so draining. They are constantly on edge and fearing the 'inevitable'. Being a carer must be like looking after a baby as depressives are as needy and dependent but even worse as they are intent on self-destruction and self-harm. If you have a carer who could benefit from talking to someone about their experiences I have set up a separate chat forum for carers on my website. Here you can also find information on the increasing number of groups available for carers.

I think this comment by a carer sums up depression perfectly; 'Just give what you have to give; because you could throw your whole life in there...depression is a black hole. It will swallow you up and still never be enough.'

When I was ill, I was selfish. When I was depressed I just couldn't help it. It is part and parcel of depression, the illness.

I don't think that there's enough help for those who are depressed never mind those who are supporting those who are depressed and who actually end up becoming their carers by default.

My husband went to a couple of meetings which took place once a week at The Priory, that were arranged for partners to meet other partners in the same situation but nothing was structured and he said that they weren't much help. Another friend of mine is going through a really tough time with depression and her husband is at a loss about how to handle her and the illness. He too has attended one such meeting but found the lack of structure and a group of partners all having the same problem desperate for help in understanding their partners and their illness thrown in a room together far from helpful.

I really do hope that this can change. Carers assume huge responsibility involuntarily and are often left and feel completely on their own and isolated. They absolve the community and the Government of responsibility and save them a lot of money but are often completely unqualified, overwhelmed and feel unable to cope. These people really need mental and physical, educational and financial support themselves. Often the carers have to give up their own jobs - and lives really - to care for their loved ones. They often end up fighting other battles with work or The Social Services for the right support or financial support on top of the emotionally and physically challenging and draining burden of being a carer.

Many of these people would not have to adopt such roles and for so long if their ‘patients’ would seek and could receive the right professional help and regularly. However, getting the right help can be and often is a battle in itself. Someone I know who is suffering from depression had to go to court because her Incapacity Benefit and her carer’s benefit had both been stopped. Neither of the two can now work due to her illness. They are struggling to live. Her husband and carer told me that he is on the edge of a breakdown himself and he is meant to be the carer.

However it may feel to you, there are ways out and there are ways to deal with and change situations, so please do not give up. There are more organisations and books now to help carers. I know several carers who have set up their own groups. See the back of this book or my website for a list of books, help and contacts.

THERAPY, MAN

I hope by now you will realise that you are not alone in experiencing depressive thoughts. Despite how isolating it feels to be depressed, therapy will teach you how to correct depressive thoughts using techniques that have been successfully developed and tried and tested in the treatment of depression.

If left to its own devices, our mind would fight our depressed feelings on its own and re-establish our mental equilibrium. Over the years we have learned many second nature thought and behaviour patterns that prevent our brains from doing that, so we need to be taught how to unlearn our negative thought patterns and replace them with better ones.

All of us develop bad habits but with determination and the right techniques, bad habits can be broken. You cannot tackle the world single handedly and when it comes to matters of the mind that is no exception. Treatment prescribed and administered by a practitioner is individual and controlled.

Therapy can sometimes be difficult to get started but don't give up. I do believe that it is possible that if you find the right therapist for you, then you can get a solution that works for you, so that you can feel strong, empowered, and positive without needing to depend on drugs. There are lots of different styles of therapies around, and I cover a lot of them in this book, so read on!

I've had enough of it and enough therapists to know. I was in therapy for seven years. Please don't think that

that automatically means that you have to spend years in therapy or a year 'on the couch' going into the depths of your personality trying to understand why you are doing something that is damaging your health. Always remember that you are in control of what you do or do not want to discuss. Be guided by the therapist who is the expert but get out of the therapy what is best for you. Take out what's best for you from what's on offer. It's all about you and for you; so you feel better; so you can feel happier; so you can get on with your life. Think about YOU and what you want.

Take my sister. She decided by herself and in her own time that she needed therapy. Being diagnosed with cancer towards the end of her pregnancy and a year of chemotherapy made her feel low.

She knew that year was the reason for her low mood. When the psychiatrist gave her the line, "Let's go back to your childhood', she replied "Don't you think the last year is enough?" She did not want or feel the need to go back to her childhood.

I wouldn't have dared say that to my therapist particularly at the beginning. She does make me laugh. I am so proud of her. She is such a strong person.

In my experience, the first, second or even third therapist may not be the right one, the therapy prescribed may not suit the individual or the antidepressant isn't helping. But one therapist or one therapy out there or one drug will be the right one. Please believe me when I say this. Please keep trying. Never give up. There is always an answer to every question in this life.

You just have to ask the right person, or look up the answer in the right book and indeed ask the right question AND VERY IMPORTANTLY AT THE RIGHT TIME FOR YOU.

Maybe you will be prescribed and find the right therapist and the right therapy first time so please don't let me give you the impression that that can't happen. It's different for everybody but if you don't, try another therapist or another therapy.

Think how many people we meet in a week or a month or even a year. How many of those people do we really like and how many become our best friends? Not many. It's not easy to find someone you would like to have as a good friend. It's the same with your therapist but it's definitely worth it to keep trying until you find a good one for you.

The right kind of therapy and therapist can find the root of the depression and cure it. Through therapy a person can have years of torment lifted and emerge happier than they have ever been. If you have had the capability to live in a happy state once, you'll do it again. I am happy to say I am.

Even if you link pain to your situation now but also link pain to change, you will stick with the familiarity of your Depression, no matter how painful it is. You may not be able to imagine any change right now. For a long time I couldn't imagine anything other than depression – apart from death. Death was the only change that I could imagine to escape from the pain. If you can link immediate massive pleasure to not being depressed, you will get better. Too much pain makes you change. Change is inevitable. One thing that we are guaranteed in life is change. Progress is not inevitable. We have to want to change for the better and to get better to make progress.

I was ashamed for a long time to tell anyone that I was seeing a psychiatrist or a Shrink as they are often referred to, albeit, light heartedly, but you know what, I have absolutely no qualms now about admitting to anyone that I see one regularly. In fact, admit seems like an inappropriate word. I don't feel I have to admit or justify myself to anyone. It helps me and my loved ones by default. Everyone has problems and everyone deserves someone totally independent and detached and objective to talk to about them.

Many celebrities have a therapist and practically everyone in Hollywood has a therapist. If it's good enough for them, it's good enough for me.

What's wrong with having someone objective to pour your heart out to when you feel overloaded, fed up, down, angry, lonely, betrayed ...? You can't just rely on your friends and family, sometimes a stranger is better.

Hey, I think everyone should have one!

Therapy doesn't just come in the form of a therapist and it doesn't just have to be therapy in the traditional sense. There are lots of things you can do to help yourself too. Go to the chapter Therapy Begins at Home to find out what about natural remedies such as homeopathy and herbal medicine.

Sometimes it is you who has to find the best cure for yourself from all that is available to you. After all, you know you best of all; better than your spouse; better than your parents; better than your children and even better than your doctor, though you should always be guided by your doctor.

Prevention is always better than cure. This is true with depression. So do all you can to avoid it? Do whatever you can to minimise the risks and your vulnerability to depression. I practise what I preach. My four things are:

I watch what I put into my body. I avoid too much stress when I can or rest after. I take herbal remedies that work well for me. Most importantly I try to do things every day that make me laugh.

If it has already happened, there is a lot you can do to correct the situation. It may not be simple. It will involve more than making a few small improvements to your lifestyle and your diet and reducing stress in your life. However, it is certainly possible to recover your life, your health, your energy, your well being and your happiness.

Therapy takes many forms.

But what is Therapy? In short, therapy teaches you the skills to help you help yourself.

Be careful of words ending in therapy though. Retail **therapy** is suspect and it doesn't do a lot for your bank balance.

My sister wouldn't recommend chemo**therapy** or radio**therapy**. They may have been her cure for her illness but they did nothing for her bald head and self-esteem so she called in back-up in the form of a psychologist for some cognitive **therapy.**

Therapy works. I used to go and have my weekly breakdown. Now I only go every six months for my 'check up'. We all know we should go to the dentist every six months for a check up. We owe it to ourselves to do the same for our minds.

THERAPY BEGINS AT HOME

Relax and be happy...

When I was depressed I felt I didn't have control over my behaviour or my emotions or my body. My behaviour was like that of a rebellious teenager in that it was destructive and unpredictable and couldn't be controlled or relied upon. My emotions were dysfunctional and unstable and created pain and fear and were out of my control. When I asked my body to do something, it refused. I was too tired. However I did have control over my thoughts.

- **Control your thoughts**

This was where my therapy started. It didn't require any energy to have thoughts. You have to think something, it might as well be a positive thought as a negative one. I could talk positively to myself. I was told I could learn to identify, prevent and correct distorted thinking and with practise manage my Depression with more rational responses to correct my negative thinking.

- **Be kind to yourself**

It is often difficult if you are depressed to do anything for yourself or treat yourself kindly, supportively and helpfully as you do to other people. You are hard on yourself when you are depressed. It helps to talk to yourself as you would to your best friend or someone else you love. Try to say to yourself the supportive, rational and accurate kinds of things you would say to your best friend if s/he felt depressed because of negative thinking.

Be truthful in your responses. You are not helping yourself or anyone else if you're not.

- **Write it down**

I kept a record of all the positive things I did. A depressed person thinks s/he does nothing right. I'd write down three positive statements at the end of each day and read them back to myself. Even if the tasks are part of your every day routine and you expect to do them well, like taking the kids to school, getting to work on time, cooking and shopping. It is important to note them as achievements. And don't forget to reward yourself with positive reinforcements.

- **Get out of bed**

Staying in bed and avoiding facing the world (as we depressives are VERY GOOD at doing!) is grasping short term relief at the cost of the long term. It all makes it so easy to give up. It really is vital that you stop saying to yourself that you are depressed and so must go to bed. Try to break this association. We've all spent days and weeks in bed and don't feel any better for it. It doesn't work so you may as well try something else!

- **Tapes**

It really takes no energy to listen to tapes that encourage positive thinking and inspire you to move forward rather than remain where you are. You can even listen to them in bed! You can stay in bed and try lots of things other than sleeping to try to lift your mood. Audio books are great. You get to be told a story! It's like your very own Jackanory. I personally guarantee that all of them will work better and make you feel better than sleeping!

You may not have the energy to go to seminars but there is so much material around you that you can have at home and work without expending too much energy.

- **Read**

It takes little effort to read, unless your Depression is so severe that reading or concentrating is difficult, and even holding a book is too much. However, when you do read, make sure that it is something positive that will help you take positive steps forward. You're already helping yourself by reading this book! Read something that will help you feel happy. If reading is too difficult, the gossip magazines are always good for a laugh - if not taken too seriously – and full of glossy pictures.

- **Talk**

Many people find it helpful sharing and talking about their feelings and depression with other people experiencing the same feelings, whether it is in a structured or unstructured environment. A friend going through a similar situation at the same time helped me.

It helps if you're not both feeling dreadful on the same day!

Some of you may feel more comfortable sharing from the comfort of your own homes on the chat forums on my website. There is lots of help on the internet where you can talk to other people in the same situation as you. If you feel up to it or you'd like to, I'd love to talk to you and you could help others on the site or find comfort yourself in talking and sharing with others. Sharing isn't for everyone though and maybe it's not right for you just now or just not right for you full stop. You know yourself and what helps and what doesn't by now, I'm sure.

- **Groups**

There are many groups already in existence that you can join or go along to when you feel like it or when you feel up to it. Most cities and large towns have Depression Alliance Groups. Many doctor's surgeries have information on such groups. The British Association of Counsellors and Therapists (BACP) and the mental health charity Mind are always helpful with providing contacts. There are also details of national and local groups on my website. I've tried many of these groups and they are helpful when and if you actually manage to get yourself out of the house and make it to the groups. You can also set up your own group at home. I advertised in the Post Office and the local paper to set up my own group. Search locally as there are probably already groups in your area and I have a list on my website.

- **Laugh**

Laughing lowers blood pressure, exercises the stomach muscles and has a profound effect on the immune system and on you. It has an amazing psychological effect on the mind and body. Watch a funny TV programme. If you feel like going out, go and see a funny film or a comedian. Laughter is a strong antidote to depression.

There is even a type of Yoga dedicated to laughter called 'Laughter Yoga'. It combines unconditional laughter with yoga breathing. Laughter Yoga is based on scientific fact that the body cannot differentiate between fake and real laughter.

- **Yoga**

There are yoga therapy classes and courses that are designed specifically for depression and anxiety but any yoga is good for depression. Yoga focuses on relaxation techniques, meditation and deep breathing that calms the mind and reconnects mind and body and promotes natural healing.

- **Use your senses**

When I was depressed I wanted total silence and didn't want to go out. It was as if all my senses which are so important for connection shut down. I cut myself off from normal sources of stimulation and pleasure.

It is important not to forget the importance of our basic senses of sight, hearing and smell and touch. What we see, smell and hear and touch can affect our subconscious more than we give them credit for.

Don't underestimate the power of a burning aromatic candle, or the uplifting effect of your favourite song. A love song is just as powerful to upset you as a bouncy song is to lift your mood. That is the power of listening.

I am sure you'll have your own 'Happy Song Archive'. Perhaps a Van Morrison number or something by Lou Reed or ABBA. I wouldn't recommend anything by Tracy Chapman, Morrissey or James Blunt![11]

- **Be at one with nature**

Gardening is great too if you like being outdoors and getting dirty. Having your hands in the soil, caring for a plant and nurturing a seed is fab!!! If you're scared of worms and frogs like I am, just make sure you always garden with a very thick pair of gloves!

Go for a walk and actually look at your surroundings. I knew I was getting better when I could appreciate the squirrel running across my path on one of the many walks my dad used to drag me out on.

The sea satisfies all our senses. The sight of the sea, the sound of the waves, you can almost taste the salt and feel the sea water on your skin. This is why we go on holiday to the sea. It makes us happy. Another bonus is that it tightens the skin, so it is also rejuvenating which is never a bad thing.

I was lucky enough to be able to move near the sea when I was ill as my parents-in-law live in a small seaside town in Scotland. I think the sea has had a lot to do with my recovery. So if you're not lucky enough to

---

[11] A study by the Cleveland Clinic Foundation revealed that chilling out to your favourite tunes for just an hour a day reduces physical suffering by up to 21% and associated depression by up to 25% and that soft music before bed may also improve your sleep by a third.

be by water, get yourselves a paddling pool or a fish tank if you're feeling down!

Most of us find water calming and therapeutic. Many of us buy water fountains so that we can have water in our gardens. Again another way to spend money. Now I know where the expression to spend money like water comes from!

Also the sun is good for us with its powerful vitamin D and daylight in general boosts your mood. This is why people suffer from the ailment SAD (Seasonal Affective Disorder) in winter or in certain countries when sunlight is limited.

- **Get a Hobby**

It is proven that hobbies ease depression and improve mood. What a great reason to do something you've always wanted to do or learn to do! Have fun!

- **Natural Remedies**

The world is full of natural cures for illness. People did very well with natural cures for thousands of years which probably explains why homeopathy and herbal medicine is gaining so much credence these days in the medical world. More and more, homeopathic and natural remedies are being used alongside conventional medical treatment. Almost any form of therapy that is in harmony with your body and the natural biological laws can help. (Refer back to 'The Happy Pills' chapter for details).

- **Pets**

I got Bess when I was ill. I knew that a dog would help me. I used to walk when I felt up to it with my dog along the sea front to the Seabird Centre and have a coffee while my dog had her well deserved bowl of water and biscuit. If the truth be known, I just gave my dog, Bess, a biscuit so that I wouldn't feel so guilty having mine.

Bess was another form of therapy for me. She got me out walking by the sea and helped me to lose weight at the same time. You don't have to buy a dog though. That is just another responsibility that when you are ill, you often don't feel able to cope with. There are lots of dog homes and pet shops and people who would welcome your dog walking services. That way you get to have a dog when you feel like it and you can hand it back when you've had a great time and had enough. Rather like the benefits of looking after someone else's child for the day!

- **Just say no**

Learning to say 'no' is good therapy and is not selfish or hostile. I'd work my butt off all week and then end up running around all weekend helping my friends. By the time it came to Sunday I had to stay up until 1 am to do my stuff. My immediate response was always 'Yes' and I'd work out afterwards how I would fit it all in and then stress about it. It is just about being realistic about your own limitations. If you learn to say 'no' comfortably, there should be no reason to fear a negative reaction from others. I still have to practise it now but am getting much better. Practice makes perfect!

- **Diet**

Diet should be an essential part of your positive DIY therapy. It is an essential element of your recovery. This is why I have dedicated a chapter to it in this book.

- **Finding your inner peace**

I found yoga and the yoga breathing and meditation very calming.

Relaxation therapies like yoga and meditation are effective in overcoming some of the other issues that can occur with depression. The effects of panic attacks, anxiety and anger can be lessened and overcome with the ability to relax properly and deeply. Physical disciplines like Tai Chi or yoga, which occupy the mind while performing gentle exercise can be useful. We did lots of Tai Chi, yoga and relaxation training such as guided imagery in hospital. It's obviously another tried and tested therapy that you might want to try. You can also get CDs or DVDs for this and do it in the comfort of your own home. You don't have to go out to a class.

Others may find solace in the simplicity of prayer.

- **Exercise**

Exercise is a potent antidepressant. Getting 30 minutes of exercise three to five times a week has been shown to be more effective in lowering depressive symptoms than taking an antidepressant alone. As I mentioned before, walking my dog got me out doing exercise and it also distracted my attention from my illness. I really enjoyed this form of exercise.

In hospital we didn't have any choice about the kind of exercise we did. It was simply part of The Programme and I didn't always like what they made us do but we all had to admit that we felt better afterwards. The key is finding something that you enjoy and choosing somewhere you feel comfortable so that you can commit to it, as the antidepressant effect of exercise wears off the moment you stop it. Every morning in The

Priory, we were summoned to 'Derek', the hunky gym instructor, in the gym for some kind of exercise, whether it was a walk, aerobics, circuit training or boxercise. You name it, Derek did it (and very well I have to say) and we followed.

How can I possibly exercise when I am depressed, exhausted and have no energy I hear you say. I am not talking about running marathons or anything extreme. I am talking about mild exercise. You already know that rest and sleep have not helped you. Undoubtedly you have tried that. If your Depression is severe, you have probably been spending a lot of your day in bed or lying around the house. This has not helped. You have slept a lot and you have almost certainly not woken up feeling refreshed and full of energy and the joys of spring.

Mild exercise helps to lift mood. Mild exercise could include walking, swimming, yoga, Pilates. Walk to the chemist to pick up your Prozac, leave the car in the garage. Don't overtax yourself. Just be content to do a little bit each day.

- **A sense of accomplishment**

Accomplishment and pleasure are incompatible with depression and an antidote to it and they divert your attention away from dwelling on your problems by engaging your mind in distracting activities. Why not cook your family a meal using a new recipe, do some painting, go out to dinner with your partner, visit a museum, tidy your home or office, clean out that cupboard (or those cupboards and stop leaving it to your friends like I used to!) or drawer you've been meaning to, go and play football with your kids in the park or try learning tennis, rollerblading or even scuba diving? The possibilities are endless. I tried most of the above (my two left feet meant that I didn't try the football and I don't have kids!). Tennis proved to be a bit of a disaster but the rest were actually real accomplishments that I am very proud of. You just need to pick one or two when you are feeling down and you will get the greatest relief from choosing something you've wanted to do for the longest time and don't forget to take a step back, admire your efforts and reward yourself.

Waiting until you feel up to doing something is self-sabotage as you will never feel up to it. Put behaviour first and your mind and mood will follow. Honestly, it will!

When I was not in my bed[12], I could be found enrolling on lots of courses. None of which were 'beneficial' as far as improving my career prospects were concerned but they filled in the time and made me feel like I was achieving something and kept me active and gave me less time to ruminate and eat.

I did a flower arranging course.
I did an interior design course.
I did a business management course.
I did an accounting course.

I was allergic to sap, had no creative flair and I think I'd rather employ someone else to manage my business and do my accounting based on those experiences!

---

[12] Although 88% of people in a medical study tried sleeping when they felt low, it was rated among the least effective methods for restoring mood. The least effective was taking a drink and medication.

- **Feel Good Products**

I also invested in copious amounts of Feel Good Products like herbal teas that promise Detox, Weight Loss, Happiness, Balance, Energy, and Relaxation. You name it and I bet that I have got a tea for it in my cupboard. Drinking tea for those things seemed like an easier option than working at it myself. My husband used to make fun of me when he made me a drink and asks me what mood I am in to determine which tea to make for me. He called me a 'marketing dream'. Don't knock it. It worked for me.

My cupboards were also bulging with shower gels and candles with all sorts of weird and wonderful claims to be 'Uplifting, Calming, Naughty' and suchlike. My favourite was 'Gloomaway' shower gel for obvious reasons. I'm sure you've got them in your cupboards too.

All these things are therapies in themselves and make therapy fun. They are therapeutic and can make you feel better. That makes them good for you. You don't feel good on the inside or the outside when you are depressed so a little help in the form of what works for you while you are in the process of sorting out both the inside and the outside, can help.

There are endless benefits from a healthy diet, exercise, beauty pampering and (to a reasonable extent) shopping. It's called retail therapy for a reason. What makes you happy, can't be bad for you, can it? As long as it doesn't break the bank or do anyone any harm.

- **Take Control**

A large part of depression is about feeling out of control and unable to control outcomes. Activities that help you to gain a sense of control - even if only in a small way -

will help reduce anxiety and improve your overall mood. While these activities are not directly aimed at your low mood, the cumulative effect of doing them will make you feel much better. They also generally require little in the way of concentration. They do however require enough attention to divert your mind from worrying and ruminating.

Don't lose control and turn to the sinister side of Therapy at Home

Some of us become dependent on more sinister kinds of 'happy pills'. Depression often goes hand in hand with the use of abusive substances, eating disorders and other addictions or addictive behaviour.

Many people 'self-medicate' with drugs, alcohol, food, shopping (as I did) or sex as they feel that these things make them feel better or ease their mental pain – for a short time anyway. However these 'drugs' give very short-term feelings of euphoria and inevitably make the depression worse. They are always followed by a terrible crash and the need for another 'fix' and yet another. This vicious circle only serves to deepen the depression.

Often people who use alcohol to ease their pain and unhappiness are labelled 'Alcoholics' and people who take drugs to ease their pain are labelled 'Drug Addicts' and people who overeat are labelled as 'fat' and judged as not taking care of themselves, and sexaholics are 'just lucky' and shopaholics have lots of nice things. I dabbled in them all and recommend none of them!

Often we are trying to increase our feel-good hormones of dopamine and serotonin with the alcohol or the food or the recreational drugs. These other abusive activities seem much more appealing, immediate and more fun and more comforting at the time.

When you weigh up the temporary high against the longer term consequences, it can be disastrous. Depressives often don't care about the long term consequences.

Things I still do at home however, and that never fail to make me feel better are: feel grateful every day; have fun and make time for fun and laughter every day even if I have to force myself to laugh to start with; eat a healthy diet most of the time; take Filisa when I'm feeling low and/or stressed; take my Vegepa omega supplements every day; make a list of my goals every day; make time for and talk to friends and family; exercise at least twice a week and on a more superficial note but nonetheless important, a trip to the hairdresser and a manicure every few months. When I was ill I didn't like myself very much and the things that I could make look good, I decided, were my hair and my nails. Everyone used to comment on my hair and nails and that made me feel good.

Don't forget the additional free therapy you get of talking to your hairdresser, beautician or even personal trainer. They are all there to help you look good and all really good listeners to help you feel better.

My sister-in-law is a beautician and is often mentally as well as physically exhausted at the end of her day from her eight massages and her constant ear bashings. It must be very draining but she loves her job and her clients and wouldn't have it any other way. She is the soul of discretion and is adamant about total loyalty to her clients.

I've listed my favourite things that work for me but you must find your own 'thing' that works for you. That something is different for everyone and again please remember, at a time that's right for you. 'One man's poison is another man's medicine'. The problem is that for a long time and definitely in the early stages of severe depression, you often simply can't do anything. That doesn't mean don't try at this stage but often nothing can get through. If you give up trying, nothing can ever get through. If you keep chipping away, something will get through.

I can hear some of you thinking out loud that the hippy in me is coming out with so many 'alternative' suggestions and you don't want to be a hippy. Well I can assure you I do not have an ounce of hippy in me and was very reassured to find that none of the alternative therapists I have visited have been draped in scarves and barefoot or 1960s throwbacks. Quite the opposite actually which made me even more receptive to their help. Not that I have anything against hippies you understand! It's a free world and all that!

In general all these self-help therapies as well as any of your own ideas will make a positive difference but most importantly don't forget to reward yourself. This might include buying or making yourself a gift, indulging in a massage or a facial, buying some fresh flowers, getting yourself your favourite food, re-reading your favourite book or anything else that is special and pleasurable to you. Rewards can also be positive things that you say to yourself and giving yourself praise instead of criticism for a change.

Do let us know what works for you on the 'Positive Suggestions' interactive feature on the website, www.depressioncanbefun.com.

EAT YOURSELF BETTER

Diet is an essential tool in your fight against depression and should be a way of life to help your mind and body function to the best of its ability to keep you healthy and alert. Diet helps rid you of those nasty toxins that have a very cruel way of showing themselves on the outside, through cellulite and bad skin, and on the inside by making you feel tired, bloated and low. If the results of bad diet are so obvious on the outside, just imagine what they are doing to you on the inside. They certainly cannot be feeding a healthy mind. You can start right now and it is guaranteed to make you feel better and look better and let's face it, if you look better you feel better anyway.

The positive therapist I was seeing as a Life Coach in Cambridge, could not emphasise enough the powers of Optimum Nutrition for the Mind and recommended that I read the book of the same name. If you feel up to it you should too.

Why is diet so important?

Because the right balance, the highest quality and the right quantity of glucose, protein and fat can beat depression. If you want to know the details of what each does look in the appendix[13].

The ideal would be to reduce or preferably to cut out all caffeine and sugar products, avoid foods that you are intolerant to, eat three main meals and two snacks every day, eat a protein source such as seeds, nuts,

[13] See Appendix 2

fish, egg, lentils, beans, meat or cottage cheese with every meal and snack and eat at least four portions of green leafy vegetables a day. I learned to do this and I can say that it made a big difference.

I would feel like I was being punished if I denied myself my morning coffee or chocolate biscuit and that really isn't the best idea. If you feel like you are being punished, you're more likely to lapse. Everything in moderation is much more agreeable with my sweet tooth and it still works. In fact, I think it works better as you are more likely to persevere until it becomes a good habit. I felt so much better when I made it a way of life rather than seeing it as a chore. It's my only good habit!

It can be difficult to receive the optimum amount of nutrition from diet alone so you may also want to consider taking a high quality multivitamin-mineral supplement. If your diet has not been great up to now and you're suffering from depression you will probably see your body and mind deteriorate at a faster rate but don't despair because you can change your diet but don't do it radically as this can be just as bad for you.

Nothing works overnight (even cosmetic surgery takes a few weeks to recover from!). Try not to be frustrated if results are slow or give up if you don't see your 'better late than never' efforts making a difference. This is going to take time and you will see results. You don't want to slip back into your old ways so be patient.

My sister was the junk food Queen. My brother used to say that her fridge contained more chemicals than 'Sellafield' nuclear power station. She lived on a diet of burgers and so many sweets I'm surprised she had any teeth left.

When the inevitable happened and she developed bulges in the wrong places, not least the 'muffin tops' and cellulite in her early 30s, she decided that she had to detox.

She started a detox that nearly killed her, literally. She detoxed so drastically that it was a total shock to her body after a terrible diet for so many years and became very ill as a result. She had pancreatitis which is usually associated with alcohol abuse but in my sister's case it was her general abuse of her body with junk and convenience food.

Such a drastic detox should really have been done under the supervision of a doctor or nutritionist.

We're all guilty of taking the easy option where food is concerned and ordering a takeaway or tucking into a microwave meal. Fresh food really takes very little time to prepare and is so much better for us. There are lots of excuses. I've used them all myself. I don't have time; I'm just too busy.

Replacing junk and convenience food with healthy alternatives, organic food if you wish, and local farm shop produce wherever possible is the best you can do for your body and mind.

It makes total sense that what you put in your body, you get out of it. How can we expect our mind and body to look after us if we don't look after them?

Here comes the science bit. It's very simple. Omega-3 in fish is good for you and your Depression. Saturated fat is bad (fried and processed food). Depression is also associated with deficiencies in zinc, selenium, magnesium and vitamins B and C. I now take these as vitamin supplements and take 'Vegepa' as my omega-3 and -6 supplement and really feel a difference (I talk more about this in my chapter on 'The Happy Pills').

I'm not a great fan of soya milk or beans and lentils or gluten free bread. However I love rice milk and rice noodles and soda bread and rye bread. I also find it time consuming and messy to eat some fruits but enjoy them just as much in a smoothie. I also love vegetable juices. Fresh juices and smoothies are great ways of getting your 'five a day' on the run. Experiment and find the healthy diet that is to your taste and that works for you.

Welcome to the benefits of chocolate

We know that bananas, apples, oranges and 'a bit of cauliflower' are good for you but the fantastic news is that high cocoa content chocolate has been proven to have feel-good factors in every bite and it's so yummy! Chocolate has been described as the non-drug antidepressant and the Prozac of plants. The serotonin and endorphins in good quality dark chocolate are good for you and your Depression.

Another ingredient of chocolate is anandamides, taken from the Sanskrit word 'ananda' meaning ecstasy, similar to the stuff in marijuana. However, you do have to eat about 25 pounds of chocolate to get the marijuana like effect. NO PROBLEM!

In fact chocolate could be described as the elixir for depression as it even releases dopamine which helps motivation.

Chocolate is also called the lust drug. I'll let you try it to find out why. Let's face it though, many women say that they would choose chocolate over sex and at least chocolate doesn't snore afterwards. I can't argue with that!

Do you need any more convincing?

CHOCOLATE IS GOOD FOR YOU! There you go, it's official. Good quality dark chocolate in moderation is good for depression.

We have smashed the myth that if it tastes good it must bad for you! I'm sure you'll find lots more that's good for you and tastes good. Have fun experimenting.

PSYCHOLOGICAL THERAPY

I ended up in therapy because I collapsed. I wouldn't recommend letting it get that far. When I have a persistent undiagnosed pain I go to the doctor, why didn't I seek help for this unknown medical condition? I knew that something was wrong.

It seems to be a different story altogether when it comes to admitting that we need emotional support and that we are not coping at work or home. It is estimated that around one-fifth of us will experience some sort of mental or emotional disorder, yet almost half of that number will not seek any help. A trip to your GP could be the start of your recovery.

Although advances in education and research have gone a long way to removing the stigma of mental illness, some people still believe there is something shameful in admitting to being depressed.

Many people's idea of therapy is what they have read about in celebrity and gossip magazines. This doesn't give them the full picture and many people are afraid of therapy because they do not know what it involves or they are worried about the possible 'can of worms' they feel therapy will open for them. Other issues people face are not having time for therapy and not having the finances or justifying the expense. But come on, you wouldn't deny yourself that handbag or the latest gadget. Is that really of more value to you than your health?

If you cannot do it for yourself, do it for those you love and who love you and depend on you and need you.

The time will be worth it and the effects of it will benefit them too and it does not have to cost lots of money.

Therapy comes from many places. It is offered on the NHS. Sometimes support and therapy is available at work through company and private medical insurance and through self-funding mental health charities like MIND. Several people I know have received therapy through such groups and have been very pleased with their support and results. Joint therapy in the form of self-help group discussions led by a group facilitator are also available free of charge from organisations like 'The Depression Alliance'. Please see the back of the book or my website for further details.

Let me just explain the forms of psychological therapy to you.

There are three basic forms of therapy. Their roles are quite different and they tend to deal with different types of problems although there is considerable overlap in their work. In summary they are:

Psychology - the study of people: how they think, how they act, react and interact.
Psychiatry - the study of mental disorders and their diagnosis, management and prevention. Psychiatrists are medical doctors who are able to prescribe medication.
Psychotherapy - helps people overcome stress, emotional problems, relationship problems or troublesome habits.

I don't want to overload your brain right now but there's more information about the different types of therapy at the back of the book[14].

Some people may use a combination of approaches at the same time. For instance, a patient may go to a psychiatrist for medication, but meet with a psychologist regularly to talk about their issues. This is the combination that I was prescribed.

As for 'shopping' for someone to talk to, I asked my family practitioner for a referral. You can also look for a social worker or therapist specialising in whatever issues you wish to talk about in local phone books, in health food shops or online. Personal recommendations are often helpful. There are directories of registered/accredited therapists. (See the back of the book for list of professional bodies). Often overlooked, local clergy can be people to ask and talk to. Community health centres and clinics frequently offer low-cost care. If you are a student or employee, it is common to have access to psychological treatment through the school or employer.

If you are feeling like you need to talk to someone outside of your immediate circle about your concerns, do consult with any of the above people. If you later feel that you don't need their services any longer, you can always cease treatment.

A referral from a GP is needed to visit a psychiatrist, whereas you do not need a referral to see a psychologist. Because of their medical training and expertise, psychiatrists are generally more expensive

---

[14] See Appendix 3

than psychologists. Very often, such medical treatment is covered by NHS or private medical insurance.

When you have sorted out whom to see and have seen them, your condition can be diagnosed by extensive medical judgment and your Depression is then given a 'label'.

- According to severity – mild, moderate, severe
- Reactive vs. Endogenous
- Bipolar Disorder
- Seasonal Affective Disorder (SAD)
- Dysthymic Disorder
- Cyclothymic Disorder
- Post Natal Depression (PND)
- Clinical Depression

If you want to know more about the labels, their details are at the back of the book[15]. People with depressive illness may also receive more than one diagnosis since the illness is often linked with other problems, such as alcoholism or other substance abuses, eating disorders, or anxiety disorders.

An insidious aspect of depression is that we tend to blame other areas of our life for how we feel. We can blame work, relationships, finances and many other things. In fact it is our treatable illness affecting our view of the world. Obtaining an accurate diagnosis and getting the most effective treatment for you, will make an enormous difference.

When I told my therapist, they figured out what I was suffering from by asking me to describe more fully my

---

[15] See Appendix 4

experiences. The therapist diagnosed the meaning of my Depression for me. That's how it works for everyone.

Don't expect this to be resolved in one session. Be prepared for it to be one step at a time.

Personally I think that too much psychiatry can be counterproductive as we can end up dwelling too much on our problems instead of moving on once we've gone over our issues and getting help with deciding how our lives can be wonderful again or wonderful in the future. I left seven years of therapy feeling sorry for myself, thinking woe is me. I have so many problems. Poor me but I've got to get out there and make the best of a bad job for the sake of those who love me and need me.

Who wants to live life like that? I certainly won't be any good to those who need me like that and I'll worry them even more with that attitude towards life and push them away. I believe there could be much more focus on helping us look forward.

The most recent and common types of psychological therapy focus on getting better. I tried one of these, cognitive therapy, which taught me new ways of thinking and acting to replace my twisted, negative thoughts and actions. I also tried traditional therapy which focused totally on my negative past. For me this didn't work as well as I felt I was just dwelling on the past and not moving forward, but it may work for you.

To cope with our lives, we have all developed our own ways of thinking. Sometimes we do not choose the best way to deal with a problem because we have distorted those ways of thinking to justify our fears.

My sister was convinced she or her son would die if she didn't keep a vigilant eye on him and that if she left him and did something positive for herself, she would get punished and one of them would die. This is distorted thinking.

After therapy, she is still overprotective as a mother but can reason with herself and allow others near her child and recognise when her thinking is a little off.

As I've said therapy worked for me. As I keep saying you need to find what works for you. Something will. Don't give up.

POSITIVE THERAPY

Positive psychology is not something I have experienced myself but I can pass on to you what I have heard and read about it.

It is becoming more popular in the US but at the time of writing this book I believe there are only two therapists currently practising it in the UK. Studies have shown that people who are treated in this way recover much quicker.

In positive therapy the therapist focuses positively on solving the patient's current problems and future wellness rather than on past hurts. The past is not ignored but the emphasis is on teaching new skills and the therapy is shorter and more focused. The therapy helps the patient to feel extremely hopeful and motivated and feel better rather than try to change their personality. There is nothing more powerful than hope in the fight against depression.

If you suffer post-traumatic symptoms, the therapist will work on removing these quickly before treatment.

A good therapist uses a combination of cognitive (see previous chapter), behavioural (along the same lines as cognitive) and psychotherapy that s/he thinks will benefit the individual the most. If the therapist thinks that it is helpful, the treatment may also include the understanding of how dreaming figures in depression which is very effective.

Psychotherapy is a good positive form of therapy as it helps people to relate to other people and express themselves. Depression sufferers often suffer and feel lack of satisfaction in relationships; both family and social. Depression can cause people to lose the skills and desire to have or be in relationships of any kind, because they want to be alone, don't know what to say or just feel bad and don't want to be in company because of poor social skills and lack of confidence.

My sister gave me a very good bit of advice for polite conversation when I was feeling totally incompetent and socially inept. She told me about: F.I.R.E. which stands for Friends; Interests; Relationships and Entertainment. This would make conversation easy when I found it very stressful and daunting to talk to people. You ask people about these aspects of their lives in turn. People always like to talk about themselves so you don't usually have to get to the end. If you do, it's time to move on anyway!

Remember that fire can spread in seconds, just like conversation can. If the fire goes out, it is time to move on to another set of people.

Often, traditional psychological therapy can go on for years. The newer positive forms of therapy have been shown to have much faster results.

This type of therapy gives you answers and solutions and the tools to fix your own problems and difficulties (even if they seem insurmountable right now), cope with stressful events better and enjoy being in control of your life both now and in the future. You will feel your spirits lift. It gives you something to be positive and be excited about. You leave a session feeling better and uplifted. You are given hope and you look forward to your future.

Once I decided I wanted to get well, I kept telling myself that I would get well which I am sure had an enormous effect on my rate of recovery. During the seven years of therapy I had when I was telling myself that it was hopeless I didn't make any progress. Once I decided that I could get better it took a year. The power of positive thinking!

I didn't read a book for four years while I was ill with depression because I couldn't concentrate and couldn't be bothered. The first book I did read was called, What Happy People Know, by Dr Dan Baker. That book proved to be an amazing turning point for me. Over the years I'd tried loads of other things like attending Depression Alliance Meetings, Initiative meetings, Positive Thinking Meetings. This book was my epiphany. I hope you find yours.

This book was humbling and inspiring. It was about an American Doctor who approaches life and his therapy through finding the positive in everyone even when everyone else has given up on it. Dr Dan Baker realised that when we are feeling appreciative of people and things around us, it is impossible to feel the fear response that makes us unhappy.

He was able to pinpoint the key things that happy people know and in doing so, developed six unique 'happiness tools' that we can use in our daily lives:

- Appreciating what we have
- Making choices
- Building personal power
- Leading with our strengths
- Telling healthy stories about our lives
- Living a balanced life

What I like about these is that they are all very 'accessible' and practical, yet far reaching things that we can do all day every day and feel better and even (dare I say it!) happy! My friend went through the list and ticked everything. She's my personal example of a happy person.

I was ready to read about other people's situations and suffering and how they bounced back from it. It had a profound effect on me. From that moment on I knew that I was ready to get better. As I keep saying timing is everything. This was the right book for me at the right time.

Two more forms of positive therapy are:
The Human Givens Approach – focuses on helping you to redesign your life to one that meets your emotional needs and uses your strengths and talents in a healthy and balanced way.

Neuro Linguistic Programming (NLP) - helps people to replace old habits and habitual thinking with good habits and thinking that is more appropriate to a balanced and happier lifestyle.

To me, positive therapy would have been the answer to my prayers and I would probably have got better a lot sooner. It plays to strengths rather than weaknesses which I think would have worked better for me. Hopefully you can access it and more positive therapists will be available soon.

Whichever path and therapy you choose you will find something that works for you. You can control your Depression. You can stop it controlling you and you will get better. I am living proof, this book is proof. I guess that makes me an expert of sorts. I’m someone who has lived through it and survived.

ECT – ELECTRO-CONVULSIVE THERAPY

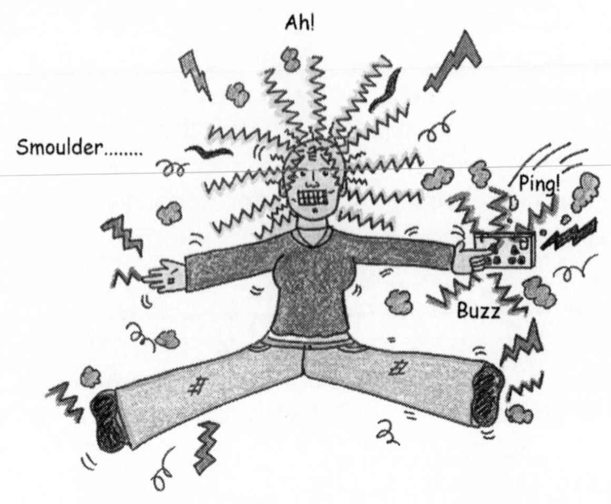

I thought that ECT warranted a chapter of its own given the controversy surrounding the treatment. It is basically a last resort method of treatment when all else fails. According to the Making Sense of ECT (1999) Mind Publication, ECT is considered a suitable treatment when it is important to have an immediate effect because, for example, a depressed person has been refusing food and drink and is in danger of kidney failure or attempted suicide.

I hope this demonstrates ECT as a desperate measure. It is after all a pretty dreadful and antiquated treatment that is unsophisticated compared to the precision of medical practice today. ECT involves passing an electric current through an anaesthetised person's brain so as to produce a seizure (fit) with the aim of relieving severe depression. Its use is highly controversial.

It was four years in to my Depression when ECT was recommended as a treatment for my Depression. I was feeling no better. Everyone could see that there had been no change, particularly my husband. In fact I was sinking deeper by the day. The tantrums had mostly stopped. I'd even given up fighting. I was just accepting of it. The first step towards getting better is Acceptance but my acceptance was Resignation. I had given up.

My husband and my doctors were so worried. The psychiatrist recommended ECT to my husband and me as the last hope. If we didn't try this, they both feared that I would never recover and would inevitably attempt suicide again.

The psychiatrist said that the procedure would shock my brain out of its depressed state. There was no technical explanation as to why it worked. The reality is that they do not really know how it works but it has been in existence as a treatment for many years as a 'last hope' measure for depression. I was told that I may suffer from short-term memory loss and that the shock treatment would shock my brain out of its negative thinking patterns that were ruining my life. The only side-effects that were mentioned were possible short-term memory loss that would return within six months. I was assured that I would not feel a thing as I would receive a general anaesthetic. A course of 13 was recommended, twice a week over a period of six weeks. We were left to think about it. I certainly was not too keen on having my brain 'zapped'. For a start I am terrified of needles and it wasn't very reassuring that no one could really explain how it worked and indeed if it would work. On top of that, I don't react well to anaesthetics and here I was contemplating signing myself up for 13 in less than two months. I must have been mad!!! I was mad. I was also desperate.

Under the Mental Health Act 1983, ECT can be given to detained patients without consent. Thank goodness, up to this point, I had managed to escape being sectioned due to my husband's determination and promises to look after me and ensure that I would not attempt to kill myself in a public place again and it was our choice to have ECT.

After weeks of deliberation, I decided that that I didn't have any other choice and I ended up having 13 awful sessions of ECT.

I remember the horror of the treatments vividly.

The morning of my treatment would arrive and my husband would have to lead me shaking, reluctant and crying downstairs to the basement room for the procedure.

Tears are coming to my eyes just thinking about the mental pain and torture of just getting myself downstairs to the treatment. I was terrified. The room looked like something you see on the television of torture chambers: The machine, the wires, the clips, the operating table, the nurses and the doctor and the anaesthetist.

My husband had to grip my hand as the anaesthetist put the needle in to my arm.

"Please let this make everything ok", I would think as I drifted into my anesthetised daze.

The next thing I would awaken on the table. All the scary looking paraphernalia was gone. Just the doctor and the nurse and my husband remained. I was helped off the couch feeling rather shaky and led back to my room.

I do not remember any pain or headaches or change of state but my husband swears that ECT saved my life. I wish I could be so sure. I just remember the horror, the fear and the pain of the anaesthetic needle (as I am terrified and tense when approached with anything resembling a needle) and feeling resentful about my 'short-term' memory loss still years after the treatment.

I still cannot remember who people are in my diary and have huge gaps in my memory of times before the ECT.

I would never agree to have it again. I still have memory loss. I suppose it depends what the doctor's definition of 'short-term memory loss' is. My 'short-term' loss has lasted years.

Depression is by far the most common diagnosis treated with ECT. Manic depression and schizophrenia were also consistently represented. Other diagnoses recorded included anxiety (2.5%), schizo-affective disorder (2%), personality disorder (1%) (I can think of a few people I would like to put forward for that!), and eating disorders (0.5%).

I had been taking medication for clinical depression for four years before ECT and had tried almost every medication there was to try. While none of them seemed to make any difference to my mood, they certainly didn't spare me the side-effects.

ECT is not a risk-free treatment either and it therefore seems particularly important that full information about side-effects should be given. In a survey conducted by Mind, the Mental Health Charity, at the beginning of January 2001, 84% of respondents to the survey said that they had experienced unwanted side-effects as a result of ECT. These ranged from short-term physical effects such as headaches, drowsiness and confusion, to permanent disabling effects on memory and cognitive function. A range of psychological effects such as feelings of worthlessness or a sense of betrayal were also reported.

The research literature on ECT does not come to a clear view on side-effects. The Royal College of Psychiatrists' Patient Fact sheet states:

"Some patients may be confused just after they awaken from the treatment and this generally clears up within an hour or so. Your memory of recent dates may be upset and dates, names of friends, public events, addresses and telephone numbers may be temporarily forgotten. In most cases this memory loss goes away within a few days or weeks, although sometimes patients continue to experience memory problems for several months. ECT does not have any long term effects on your memory or your intelligence."

However, other research suggests that memory loss can persist and that this is different from the memory loss caused by depression.

My sister keeps referring to things that we did together before my ECT of which I have absolutely no recollection.

When we were on the escalators on the London Underground together for the weekend that she won The Positive Mother of The Year Award and we were passing the posters of all the musicals, she commented on going to see 'Lion King' the musical. "Oh, that's nice", I replied. "Who did you go with?" To which she replied "You, you idiot!"

The poor girl also sold her motorbike to be able to afford to take me to a health farm for a break when I was initially diagnosed with physical and mental exhaustion. I have absolutely no recollection of this either much to her disappointment and mine!

I read an article in the paper about, the actress and comedienne, Caroline Aherne having ECT for her Depression. The side-effects listed in the article stated permanent memory loss, confusion, difficulty in concentrating and paranoia as side-effects of the treatment.

I have been battling with the psychiatrist who recommended the treatment to acknowledge these side-effects and particularly the permanent memory loss but he only ever admitted temporary short-term memory loss. I was worried that it was just me. I still have huge gaps in my memory. I do still hope that my memory comes back and I remember and recognise events and names in my diary as believe me, only people worth remembering make it into my diary, which makes it even more frustrating!.

I hope that this demonstrates that ECT is not a risk-free treatment but then few treatments are. I wish that I had had more information to hand when making my decision on whether to proceed with ECT. I leave it to you to make up your own mind.

DEPRESSION – DENIAL

My Depression started early on in my new job. I was so desperately unhappy. I used to cry all the time in private. I used to cry all the way to work and from work; I used to cry myself to sleep; I used to wake up and cry. I used to self-harm by beating myself and hitting my head either with my fists or against the wall so hard that it would hurt.

I was trying to punish myself but I was also trying to make my mental pain physical as I can handle physical pain but I could not handle my brain hurting. It was totally unfamiliar to me. I had never experienced such mental pain. I did not know what to do with it. I just did not know what to do full stop. I didn't know how to ask for help or whom to ask for help or what to ask for help for.

I withdrew from social contact. I was totally preoccupied with my fears, my thoughts and my problems. I knew this about myself and that is why I felt that I would not be 'good company' if I went out when feeling low.

When I tried to go out with my husband and socialise, the contrast between my thoughts and the gaiety around me would just deepen my low mood.

I started to self-loathe, both my body and myself as a person. I started pretending to feel ill when we were supposed to be going out and I used to send my husband by himself. This went on for almost a year before even my husband realised the reason. He started to call me on my way home from work and I would be crying. Then the crying turned into not getting out of bed at the weekends; not wanting to go out with our friends or have people to stay. Then it spiralled into threatening over the phone on my way home from work that I was going to throw myself in front of a bus. Even then I couldn't see the problem.

At this stage, I hadn't moved to the next and worst level of depression. The reason I didn't throw myself in front of the bus is because I didn't want to ruin the bus driver's life by them witnessing such trauma.

When I was at my worst, there was no such reasoning, just a need to die. I just wanted to die. My wish for death was so strong. I used to plummet so very quickly into feelings of hopelessness and despair. I used to feel that I was responsible and 'to blame' for the way I was feeling and believed that others would be better off without me.

There was no consideration for who may be distressed by seeing my suicide.

I even trawled the internet about getting to the countries that I know tolerate voluntary suicide. Obviously this is for terminally ill patients but that didn't stop me investigating and thinking that they would make an exception for me. My husband found out by looking at my computer which put him under more pressure to keep the doors and windows locked.

That's when my husband took me to the doctor. They told me that I was mentally and physically exhausted (which pretty much covered it at that time) and she told me to go away for two weeks and rest, with antidepressants of course! Prozac. My goodness. That stuff should be marketed as a hallucinogenic. I felt like I was floating everywhere. A terrible feeling. Off the wall.

Two weeks later there was no change so they admitted me to a private clinic in Windsor under a psychiatrist who I didn't feel particularly comfortable with. They changed my drugs. Now I was just feeling sleepy and numb. This seems to be how a lot of antidepressant drugs make one feel.

I was scared of all the repercussions of admitting that I had a problem and stopping my life in any way. I was scared what people would think and how they would react. After all, I was disappointed in myself and embarrassed and ashamed so how could I possibly expect everyone else's reaction to be any different to my own? I preferred to carry on and pretend that all this wasn't happening. I was still in denial.

Please, if you're at the level one stage of depression that I was talking about, stop, look at your life, ask for help, if you feel able, or are able to change what it is that is upsetting you and making you so unhappy. If you can take a holiday, take one. If you can't take a holiday, take a step back to see if you can make it any more bearable; go and see your GP; call someone, chat to other people either at self-help groups advertised locally or at your doctor's surgery, or chat on my website forum to other people or to a therapist on my website.

I don't want you to have to go to the next stage like I did. I am lucky enough to be coming out of it despite two attempts to take my own life, but many aren't so lucky and never get to the other side to have a chance to see the light.

It is sometimes said that if you try to kill yourself in a public place, you want help, that it's a cry for help and selfish as you involve other people and waste the time and money of the public services. Sometimes it is a cry for help yes, but as I have already said, some people have gone way past caring about a cry for help and being noticed. They just have an overwhelming need to end the pain and suffering and the only way that they see of doing that is to die. It's a terrible feeling.

Unless someone has experienced that feeling they will never understand or be able to understand and how could we expect them too. That feeling of driving and wondering what would happen if you just drove off the road and over the cliff. Would that really be it? Would that be an end to the suffering? Or when you are walking along the street crying your eyes out with an overwhelming desire to throw yourself under a bus or on to the train track, would that really stop the living hell?

You begin to find ways and 'opportunities' of killing yourself as you go about your everyday life in the most unlikely and unusual situations and places. Things you do every day like taking the kids to school, walking to and from work and making dinner become an 'opportunity'.

Even the fact that I wanted to die didn't make me accept that I had a problem. I would rather have died than face up to the fact that I was ill. I couldn't face what that would mean.

If you don't accept something as a problem, how can you ever be in a position to find the solution? I would have gone on if my husband hadn't taken me to the doctor. I could not accept my Depression. I didn't know it as depression then. I didn't really know what depression was to be able to describe what I was feeling as depression, having never experienced and suffered anything like this in my life before.

I kept the doctor and my husband happy by taking a rest in a private hospital and taking my prescribed meds but checked myself out after two weeks and went back to work and carried on along the road to rack and ruin until I physically collapsed and was forced to ACCEPT.

THE STIGMA

No one else understood or acknowledged my fear of the stigma of depression. I resented the diagnosis and the label of depression that I feared would mean the end of my life as I knew it and tarnish my CV and reputation for ever.

My husband was so worried about me that he even went to see my boss at his house while he was on holiday to express his fears about my workload and deteriorating state of mind. He didn't tell me but boys being boys and their toys, he let it slip about my boss's new red Ferrari on his drive. "How do you know about that?" I asked him and then he told me. Bless him!

I was angry at the time as I did not want anyone to know that I couldn't cope. I was worried that I would lose respect as a professional, that I would lose my job and my pride. Little did I know that I was going to lose a lot more than that, like my sanity for starters!

As far as I was concerned, no one could know why I had been off work for six weeks. That would be my career in tatters. Everything I had worked for since leaving University. I was distraught at the prospect of my work colleagues – most of them being men – knowing and thinking that I could not stand the pressure of work and that I was actually 'depressed'. I could not admit to feeling depressed, especially being one of only a few women in a male dominated environment. I just couldn't.

They wouldn't understand. How could they? Why would they? I didn't understand it before I became ill with depression.

It was agreed with my doctor that my sick notes would be submitted with the diagnosis as: 'Viral Infection'. This in itself was to come back and haunt me in a court case and caused the whole medical system of writing accurate sick notes to be changed by law. Little old me pissing off all future patients with illnesses they do not want their bosses to know about and causing the medical profession another headache.

My sister's friend who is a doctor told me that surgeries had been instructed to comply with new stricter regulations regarding the writing and submitting of accurate sick notes following my court case and the judge picking up on an incorrect sick note as a reason for my subsequent inappropriate treatment at work.

How bad did I feel? This was just another bit of guilt to add on to my already burdened shoulders that I had been adding to every day since day one of my Depression. It was a pretty heavy list by now too I can tell you. This time it was very real and worth worrying about as it was plastered all over the newspapers every day for a week during the court case. At least it made this guilt real and very justifiable to worry about!

I kept on going for another nine months in a terrible state. I had started to refuse phone calls from anyone and hid in bed all weekend and just got up on Monday mornings to commute to work and would then work and stay in London all week and come home to my husband at the weekend. I do not know how I kept it together at work but nobody knew or seemed to know and I actually managed to act normally on the trading floor and do my job. This seems to happen in a lot of cases.

I was under a lot of pressure at work and a lot was expected of me. The more I did, the more was expected of me. The more you demonstrate you can do, the more others demand of you. People expect it. You become a victim of your own abilities. I couldn't say no to people. I had tried to delegate but things did not seem to get done as I wanted them to be done. I therefore became reluctant to delegate or cut back on my workload. I knew that I was stressed but I saw it as a weakness to give in.

The prolonged distress – mental and physical exhaustion – nervous and emotional disturbance, insomnia, heart palpitations, anxiety, irritability, stomach pains and depression were just eating me away. If I didn't conquer this myself, I would be disappointed in myself. My self-esteem would take a dangerous plunge.

No one ever really speaks about depression. Despite progress, it still seems to have a stigma attached to it and you only become a member of the 'club' or find out who's suffering or suffered from it when you 'get it'. It's a bit like the Impotence club or the Stress Incontinence club! Unless you've got it or done it, you never know about it or hear about it!

You are unlikely to be the obvious choice if you get narrowed down to the top two for a job when your job application is 'blotted' with the word depression. That's just the way it is for the moment. It's sad and unjustified given my previous examples of many great people of past and present who have been or are 'blighted' by depression. You may be thinking 'how do I overcome that?' Well there is lots of advice on my website that can help.

A male friend of mine who is a senior manager for a large retail company and manages over 100 people, has said to me, that he doesn't "get the depression thing", and dismissed it as feeling sorry for oneself.

Someone asked me at a coffee conference why I was opening 'Mood Cafes'. When I told him that I had suffered with depression for a long time myself and was wanting to help others, he said that he was surprised that I had 'admitted' to suffering from depression as in his experience not many people talk about it. I was simply answering his question and didn't see it as 'admitting' to being ill.

People handle things in different ways but it does show that as a nation, still relatively little is understood about depression as an illness. It is a sad fact that we are more sympathetic to physical illness but it is not hard to see why. It is still seen as an excuse or a sign of weakness by many and not surprisingly such a stigma keeps many people suffering in silence.

Even in this day and age, depression is still stigmatised. At the other extreme, the perception to some people is that it's trendy because celebrities are publicised and glamorised for being treated for depression and photographed going into The Priory or Rehab. It's probably helping people's acceptance if not their understanding of depression. Unfortunately this belittles depression. I am sure that if you ask any depressive about their illness, you won't find the word 'trendy' anywhere in their description.

When someone who thinks they're helping tells you to pull yourself together, don't let it upset you or hold it against them. They don't understand that if you could you would. Nobody wants to feel down. It's a feeling you wouldn't wish on your worst enemy. I just wanted to die and spent all my time planning how I could kill myself. I didn't care about leaving anyone behind and how they would feel because in my negative thinking, they'd all be better off without me. I had no doubt about that. I felt sure that they were embarrassed by me and that I was a burden to everyone. I couldn't handle the thought of the Stigma. Depression totally warps the mind.

Given that stress and depression have overtaken back pain as the most common reason for people being off work sick I do hope that this means the help and support on offer will keep getting better.

A very good friend of mine watched an excellent programme on depression that gave her a much clearer understanding of the illness which made me feel much better because she has witnessed some pretty weird stages of my Depression that could have meant the end of many of my friendships if my circle of friends hadn't been so true, loyal and understanding.

My mood swings were extreme, my conversation morbid, my periods of isolation were long but more specifically I went through an extreme and dangerous and unacceptable promiscuity during my manic episodes. After six whole years of absolutely non-existent libido or 'mojo' as my friends and I refer to it, I really could not explain it any other way as it was totally out of character. Many people say it was an excuse but I really did not know what was happening to me as if I had, I would not have done it as it totally wrecked my marriage with the man with whom I thought I was going to spend the rest of my life.

Knowledge and awareness can only help with the Stigma attached to depression. I hope that this and other programmes like it will find prime time screening time very soon. It does appear to be getting better but there's room for improvement.

DEPRESSION - YOU INHERITED IT

Are we born with The Black Dog of Depression?

My dad has a magnet on his fridge that was bought for him years ago by his sister, herself a mother of two, that says 'INSANITY IS INHERITED – YOU GET IT FROM YOUR KIDS'.

Well, my doctor and my husband were convinced that I inherited my Depression from my mother. I was initially diagnosed as suffering from genetic depression as my mother's father killed himself and my mother found him and then she did the same thing when she was 39 years of age.

I don't know the circumstances of my grandad's suicide. I never met him as he too died young. We don't even really know the reason for my mother's suicide though I have my own thoughts. There wasn't the mental health awareness or support back then that there is today.

My husband and I had very strong disagreements over this diagnosis and it was he who first suggested to the doctors, that he thought that my Depression was genetic.

Eventually the doctors agreed that my Depression was circumstantial or EXOGENOUS as the psychiatrists call it officially, which is depression as a result of outside factors. Factors such as divorce, job loss, money troubles, stress or the death of a loved one, but stated somewhere in my file is the fact that I could have indeed been predisposed to it due to a family history. I do wonder if I hadn't been so closely involved with suicide, if it would never have entered my mind to be a real possibility or a way out. But I know people who have tried to kill themselves who haven't got a family history of depression so who knows?! I guess I'll never know but I don't feel the need to know and I do not feel that knowing would change my situation.

However, I do not doubt that the relevant gene that causes depression or the negative chemical imbalance that can cause depression, can be inherited just the same as a physical gene can be inherited.

I have often heard 'Depression runs in our family' or 'It's in our genes' as comments about causes for depression.

There is some evidence according to medical research that depression has a genetic basis, in particular Manic Depression or Bipolar Disorder.

However

1. It has also been proven that most depression is learned, not genetic. (1)
2. Because much depression has to do with styles of thinking, behaviour and interpersonal relationships, it is much more likely that depression styles are passed down in families by learning. (2)
3. Even if you do have a genetic predisposition to depression, it is no more than a predisposition. You are not certain to become depressed. There is no gene for depression, and there never will be because genes just don't work that way.(3,4)[16]

It is hard not to be affected by a depressed person and as children, much of our behaviour is learned from parents. I don't remember my mother being depressed but then again I wasn't aware what depression was as a child, so I wouldn't have recognised the signs. As a teenager with attitude, I would probably have interpreted any negative behaviour as normal mother/daughter conflict. I do remember being quite difficult for my mother but then again how many pleasant, well mannered, obliging teenagers do you know? Exactly! Unfortunately for teenagers, the hormone, oxytocin, that

---

[16](1) Yapko, M.D. (1998) Breaking the Patterns of Depression. Bantam Doubleday Dell Publishing Group; Main Street Books ed edition.
(2)Yapko, M.D. (2000) Hand-ME- down Blues: How to Stop Depression from Spreading in Families. St Martin's Press Inc.
(3)Papermaster, DS. (1995). Necessary but insufficient. Natural Medicine. 1, 874-5
(4)Le Fanu. J. (1999) The Rise and Fall of Modern Medicine. Little, Brown & Co.

makes a parent's love unconditional from birth, has worn off by now and parents start giving as good as they get.

Indeed, thinking about it, my Depression does seem to have coincided with the time in my life that my mother's depression was diagnosed. Maybe it is a coincidence. Maybe it coincided with a time in our lives when we thought we should be somewhere else or happier or richer or younger. I do not know if my grandfather was of the same age when he killed himself but he must have been a young man in his thirties at least for my mother to have found him when she herself was a girl.

Whatever I think, the 'genetic depression' label remains in my file and I had to settle for that as I am no medical expert to argue (even though I tried!). I do however know my own personality. I think that I have coped quite well. Up until now I had coped with the sudden early death of my mother in my early teens and then coped at home with a father, who for quite some time wanted to follow his wife and became very ill and low himself after being the most positive man in the world for ever and a day.

He was at the same time trying to build a business and would entertain clients at home in the evening with my fledgling attempts at cooking for them (with a very slow coal-driven AGA with a mind of its own). I remember quite enjoying it and seeing it as a challenge.

I tried to look after my little brother who needed nurturing and raising. Actually by the age of 10 he was so independent that it used to make me cry that such a young boy was forced to grow up and become so responsible and independent so quickly that he refused to let me do his ironing or even make his school lunch box up! He has always been and still is a complete gem of a brother and never any trouble to anyone.

I also had a wayward middle sister who completely went off the rails smoking and hanging around with a 'bad crowd' and ended up leaving school without any qualifications and moving out of home just to get away from an extremely difficult relationship with her dad, at the age of 16 to live with a violent boyfriend, who actually ended up stabbing her. Given all that, I think I am quite a strong and well balanced person. I think we all are and we are very close.

I did my O levels, A levels, went to University and got my first job shortly after graduating.

So despite the 'difficulties', I seemed to sail through all this and got on with it. I tried to be quite logical about it. It is nature's way that the parents should die before their children. The other way around is worse. I cannot imagine how terrible it is to lose a child. In the animal kingdom, the young are left to fend for themselves almost immediately. Humans are unique in their dependency on parents beyond weaning. I was quite capable of looking after myself now. I wouldn't have chosen to obviously.

I was trying to convince my doctors and my husband for that matter that if I were prone to depression and had a genetic disposition to it then surely this period would have triggered it. They weren't having any of it though.

I felt that I had a healthy mindset and nice memories about my mum and I had a very supportive dad. My mum had always been keen for me to study languages which I wanted to do anyway so I took German at school in addition to the compulsory Spanish. Another good thing about taking German was that I avoided the embarrassment of sex education at school to do it! I went on to study languages, politics and economics at University. I've always been interested in fashion and knew I wanted to work in the fashion industry so when I left university I joined 'LIF' London International Fashions so I could combine my languages with fashion. Perfect! I felt quite good about that too because not only had my mum wanted me to study languages, she had loved fashion too.

Unfortunately the company went bankrupt a year after I joined. Nothing to do with me I hasten to add!

By a total fluke, I went to see an agency I liked the sound of and they said that I would be ideal for a position that they had at a large American Investment Bank in the City on the trading floor. Six interviews later and a final interview in front of a panel, which all seemed very daunting, I got the job. Then it was the call to father. 'Ooh I don't know whether I want it. Trading. In London. Little old me.'

My dad very kindly said that there would always be a job for me at his company and that I should go with my heart. I think that I have taken that advice a little too readily a little too often and I use it all the time to make my decisions. The results have never been as good as when I applied them to the only time he actually told me to use it for that situation but anyway it was the best thing I ever did and it allowed me to fulfil one more dream: to own a convertible sports car.

I was headhunted and moved on from that company that had made me very happy and successful and had made me feel secure and like part of a big family. My memories of being happy end there really. As far as I recall, I was never happy again. I lost my focus. That's when I lost me.

THE PRIORY

Then I found myself in The Priory; the Five Star Hotel of Roehampton. Lots of famous people are always in there, some have been in there several times. I was in there twice. What is my point? My point is, is it working?

Mind you, only recently I was thinking how an escape there for a couple of weeks would be quite nice if only my medical insurance hadn't run out! Maybe that's what it is. It's an escape, not necessarily a cure. An escape from this harsh world we all find ourselves struggling in. You feel safe in there.

It's a beautiful building in beautiful grounds (not that I got to explore it much). So it should be as they certainly charge Five Star rates. I would have struggled if I'd had to pay for room and board myself. What am I talking about? I did eventually have to pay their rates for several weeks as my private health care stopped paying. It cost thousands of pounds.

I wasn't aware of a lot going on around me when I was in the Priory but I do remember my room as being very bland and it appeared to me to be very dull and grey. My husband tried to brighten it up by sticking photos on the walls of us doing nice things together. Of course my memory of it could have a lot to do with my state of mind at the time. Even if it had been decorated like a Disney palace it probably wouldn't have made any difference.

The single metal framed bed was tucked under a window in the corner of the room. Normally a bed near the window is my preference so that I can look out but I spent most of my time in bed with the curtains closed so the window was an unnecessary luxury. There were bars against it anyway so it felt a bit more like a prison to me so I wasn't bothered that I couldn't see it. I only used to come out when I had to for group therapy and to eat. I didn't like having to come out and I didn't like group therapy or communal eating.

I just wanted to be on my own in my room and more specifically in my bed. I was much happier when my therapist or psychiatrist used to come into my room to see me. I felt much more at ease when they did that. I would rather have eaten in my room too but we weren't allowed to take food in our rooms. We all had to eat in the communal dining room which I remember being equally as bland as my room.

I enjoyed the food as the choices I made reminded me of school dinners. With hindsight, I just put on even more weight as a result of all the fish and chips and sticky toffee pudding I ate. Knowing what I know now, all that sugar and fat wasn't helping my Depression.

Forget "Healthy body, healthy mind" and "What you put in you get out", I wasn't even capable of choosing whether I wanted tea or gin and tonic in the mornings, never mind a three course meal. Being given the option to eat unhealthily when we are not in a position to look after ourselves was not the best idea. Of course I was going to eat everything that was bad for me. It is important that people in hospital eat well to keep their immune systems strong and keep up their strength to fight illness.

When my sister was in hospital seriously ill with an infection during her chemotherapy treatment for cancer, the food was of really poor quality and could have contained no nutrients in the state that it arrived. Its purpose was merely to provide a meal. I used to prepare food and fresh juices at home to take in for her.

I really do hope we see an improvement in this situation very soon.

Stimulants like tea and coffee are never in short supply though. Often when you are ill or depressed, you crave stimulants and anything bad for your body really. Why do we always crave what is bad for us? I suppose because they taste better or because they are what we are used to tasting better.

Too much cortisol, otherwise known as the 'stress hormone', due to too much stress, can create cravings for salty and sweet foods. Cortisol was a very good adaptive mechanism that helped us stock up on supplies in the dark ages when we hunted for our food but in our modern society it just adds to our waistlines!

The TAI CHI, painting (when I haven't got a creative bone in my body), baking, boxing classes, team games and the rest of The Programme for that matter, only served to depress me even more as I couldn't do it, any of it! I had no energy, no concentration, no enjoyment and no social skills and absolutely no interest. I remember my sister saying that I could do flower arranging and I spat back that I had a degree, why on earth would I want to waste my time with that and I am not artistic anyway. I wasn't attacking her; I was actually attacking my fear. Secretly, I didn't want to make myself look even more stupid than I felt. I didn't feel that I could do anything but I didn't want anyone else to know or see that.

I was never very communicative in the classes and group therapy classes. I preferred one to one therapy just because I felt so low and didn't feel that I could cope with lots of people around me.

I did meet some really nice people the second time I was in there when I wasn't quite as self-obsessed. I still keep in touch with one or two and am pleased to say that they are doing well.

Really, the only thing I used to look forward to was my husband bringing my coffee in or on a special occasion, taking me out for my cappuccino (good to know that that sense didn't go). I craved coffee terribly. When I look back at my diary, my highlight of my day used to be my husband coming in to bring me a coffee. Life really isn't meant to be like this folks.

It's a shame that I don't even remember the one thing that I used to look forward to during my illness due to my short-term memory loss from so much 'electric shock treatment' while in there. I still find it frustrating that much of the detail of the four years of my Depression before the ECT is missing because of the short-term memory loss that is a common side effect of the ECT treatment. My doctors told me that it will come back, but I'm still waiting!

I only know some of the events of the last years because of the diary that I was encouraged to keep while I was in The Priory by my cognitive therapist in her quest to aid my recovery and from talking to my family and friends. I really did and still do find this very useful and that's why I suggested that you might try it.

I say 'her quest': I actually didn't want to get better. I just couldn't see myself ever getting better. In my mind, things could never get back to how they were, i.e. the perfect distorted image I had of my past life. Anything less than that just wasn't acceptable and I knew that I would never be able to have my old life back as I had lost my career; all my trading exams that took years to complete had lapsed and I felt that I didn't have the brain or concentration capacity or time and money to do them again; my husband and my friends (or so I thought) had gone and I was not half the person I had been. I just wanted it all to end. I could not face carrying on like this. I just signed my own death warrant really.

You know that light at the end of the tunnel that everyone talks about? Well, a depressed person's tunnel is never ending and oh so black, more like the black hole.

A depressed person doesn't believe in light, they really don't. We think that those people who believe in light, don't know what they're talking about when they tell us and try to convince us and reassure us that there is light at the end of the tunnel. "They don't understand. How can they know my life, my thoughts, and my Depression? I'll never see the light again". The brain is such a complicated thing, especially a woman's of course as my husband (most husbands) will tell you!

There are so many doctors out there and so many psychiatrists and therapists and counsellors. I am none of those but I have had a lot of experience of all of them. It is good to talk about a problem to get it out in the open, off your chest, talk it through with someone who understands, a good listener and who does not judge. These people don't tell you what to do but are excellent listeners and do not jump in with their own advice which can be so annoying especially when even the advice family, friends and people are giving you isn't what you want to hear. I did a lot of talking, getting things out in the open and getting things off my chest when I was in The Priory.

THE NHS MENTAL INSTITUTION

My husband had managed to avoid having me sectioned twice before by admitting me voluntarily to The Priory. I had had no idea that there had been any danger of this. I was completely oblivious to anything that was going on around me, except my own pain.

Unfortunately the last time I tried to kill myself, I was not so lucky. I ended up in hospital to get my stomach pumped and that is where the State stepped in and sectioned me. Control was taken out of my husband's hands as the public emergency services had to get involved and I was sectioned and as my medical cover had run out, I woke up sectioned in the NHS mental institution.

I now know that I am very lucky.

Luckily, suicide didn't work for me and I am still here with the opportunity to rebuild my life but when I woke up and was aware of my surroundings, I certainly didn't consider myself lucky.

Last time I tried to kill myself, I decided that the building I had tried to jump off last time wasn't high enough. I knew that as I had stood on top of it and looked down. At best a broken arm I thought. At worst, paralysed and then that would be even worse as people would have to look after me permanently and I wouldn't be in a fit state to try again. I wanted to stop being a burden to everyone, not be an even bigger one.

This time I was determined to find a building high enough to secure my fate once and for all and put an end to the pain in my head that would not go away, and an end to the hopelessness and deep sadness that I just could not escape. I scoured Edinburgh.

This time I planned to jump off the roof of my favourite department store in Edinburgh, which happens to have a restaurant on the very top floor. It's quiet there in the evening midweek when the store is closed and just the bar is open. I'd go there.

I planned my outfit carefully. Casual Evening Attire. Every hair in place. Make up had to be perfect. Why, I really don't know. I think that at the back of my mind I just wanted to look beautiful and at peace in the end after all the pain. I think that's what it was.

I drove to Edinburgh from my house which was about 40 minutes out of town. The journey is a complete blur to me. I parked (I can't remember where) and made my way to the top floor and ordered a Kir Royale; my favourite drink. I remember that bit. Then for some reason I ordered another and another and then I remember a bottle arriving at my table in an ice bucket but don't remember ordering it or what it was. My mind was a mess. There were too many people around and I wanted to wait until the bar was quieter.

I thought that I had better leave a note apologising to my family and my husband for all the upset I had caused them. I didn't think about the trauma they would face when I was gone. I thought that I was doing everyone a favour by leaving. The note was very emotional. Writing it really upset me. That's when I remember taking the Valium tablets that I had in my handbag that I had picked up that afternoon as part of my prescription.

Before I knew where I was, I had taken all three boxes. I don't remember anything after that and I didn't wake up until I was in a mental hospital. Yet another mental hospital but this time it was an NHS hospital. Oh my goodness was I in for a shock.

Apparently my husband's best friend (who's a pilot) took to the skies in his plane to scour the countryside for my car. Everyone was out looking for me.

To this day I do not know how my sister-in-law came to find me on the floor in the ladies of the bar in a pool of my own sick (very nice!) and rush me to hospital. Poor girl still can't bring herself to show herself on the top floor in that store. She still has the clothes she found me in at the very bottom of her ironing pile. She never did like ironing!

Added to the distress of taking me to hospital, my husband and sister-in-law were very offended when they arrived at the hospital to be asked if they were my parents.

My husband apparently scolded the nurse for her presumption and told her that she wasn't looking too great herself.

My sister-in-law tells me that she remembers being left with my handbag and thinking how she had never held a Lulu Guinness handbag before and how beautiful it was. In fact she was thinking how this was probably the only time she would ever hold one and quite liked it but how bizarre that it should be at A&E with her sister-in-law!

Apparently I had my stomach pumped at the hospital which I am very pleased I was unconscious for. I then had to be escorted to and from the ambulance that took me to the mental hospital by a bouncer because the hospital feared that I would try to escape. I don't even remember being conscious so heaven's knows how I would have escaped. I don't remember any of this. I only learned later of the hospital and the bouncer when my sister and I were talking.

When I woke up my sister was by my bed. My husband wasn't getting on with my family at the time as they disagreed on the cause of and treatment of my illness. Apparently my sister had gone against his wishes and snuck into the hospital without him to see if I was ok.

She had driven up from Nottingham against my husband's wishes as soon as she had learned from my father's fiancée what had happened. My father was away on business again and his fiancée had taken the call from the hospital. In a panic, she called my sister who jumped in her car, sped four hours up the motorway and burst into my room at the hospital only to be curtly escorted off the premises under the instruction of my husband.

Obviously I was totally unaware of all this as I was unconscious and only woke up some 24 hours later 'sedated and sectioned' in the dreadful NHS mental hospital.

Two things that I never want to be ever, ever again.

It had to be at the NHS hospital that they sectioned me didn't it. Why couldn't it have been at the Five Star BUPA Hospitals in Windsor or London where I had ended up before? They were much more my cup of tea! Much more anyone's cup of tea I'm sure! It was scary I'm telling you but, then again, I think that this was a turning point that I was ready for.

I was never coming back here again.

I thought The Priory was bad but at least there were famous people in there and Derek the LA gym instructor was a hunk. Despite losing my libido, I could at least still appreciate his beauty from a distance so I knew that I wasn't totally beyond repair!

Depression is very real. Those of us going through depression or who have been through it know that but eventually and at some time, normally as you are coming out of the worst of the depression, there can be an element of self-pity.

This stage coincided with my being sectioned in Herdmanflat Hospital, the NHS mental institution and this time I was ready for the kick up the arse realisation that I never ever wanted to go back to this place or any place like it ever again.

As soon as the morning came and I came around after my suicide attempt, something changed in me, in my head. I wanted to live and I wanted to get better. No one believed me. The nurses didn't believe me, my husband, family and friends didn't believe me, but my new NHS psychiatrist did believe me. There's a turn up for the books. A doctor believing me! There's apparently some theory that he and a specialist from the Royal Infirmary in Edinburgh had written a controversial paper about, that backed up my complete and sudden turnaround. I was text book. Thank God. It has something to do with the shock of totally unexpectedly waking up after a suicide attempt and almost having an epiphany like experience and really appreciating the seriousness of the situation. I could hardly believe the change in myself. I'd wanted to die, I tried to die, I didn't think I cared and then I woke up and I was in hell, I did care, very much.

I was through the stage of just wanting to end it all and, I then switched to being desperate again. This time, I was desperate to feel better.

I just wanted someone or my psychiatrist or a psychic, come to think of it, to give me the answers. I used to think to myself that if someone could just tell me what to do to get better and guarantee that it would work, I would do it, whatever it may be. I was willing to do anything. I really was.

The answers do have to come from within I'm afraid as I learned eventually. I know you might think that's just not possible, you're just not capable. Maybe you're not, right now. Time is a great healer. I promise you that one day you will be able to. Be patient if that cure or treatment is offered at the wrong time for you and doesn't seem to be working. It will work when you're ready for it.

Because my psychiatrist believed that I was his text book case he was willing to let me out of the hospital after two weeks but under the supervision of my husband, but my husband said 'No'. He said that he didn't think I was ready to be released.

My husband who was supposed to love me and care for me said no!

I just saw red and went for him. Can you imagine my reaction at the thought of more incarceration in that place? He had no idea what it was like in there. My mother-in-law has told me how she used to cry in her car when she had to leave me in that awful place. So many mental hospitals have closed in recent years and this was the only one left in East Lothian. All types of cases were just flung together in mixed wards. Delinquents, OAPs with senile dementia who care homes refused to take, manic depressives, clinical depressives, schizophrenics; you name it, all of us together.

One guy, who scared the living daylights out of me, had been there since 1967. That's my birth year for God's sake. How can they put someone that institutionalised together with such transient patients as me? Well, I was hoping to be more transient than I actually was!

He used to call me 'Blondie' and tell me how much he wanted to 'shag' me over the table which I can tell you was a terrifying thought. I reported it to the nurses but what could they do. They probably thought I was a stuck up snob from England who needed to be taught a lesson anyway. Actually, that's not fair, most of the staff were nice and after all, their job must be pretty impossible much of the time. It was unfortunate that the member of staff I spoke to wasn't nice and sympathetic when I was declaring my fear of being raped but then again maybe I wasn't very nice, I don't remember.

I remember the poor guy who I was assigned to after my admission to the NHS hospital when my designated psychiatrist was away on holiday for two weeks.

I wanted to go out to get my nails manicured – as you do! He would not let me leave the hospital despite my promises to go there and come straight back (who could blame him given my track record to date).

My nails were the only thing I actually liked about myself at that time (I am sure we have all felt like this at some time or another girls), and the poor guy winced at my verbal retaliation. "Are you married?" I screamed. He meekly replied that he wasn't married. Not that it was any of my business and he would have been totally justified not to answer. I carried on screaming. "Well you never fucking will be as you don't understand a woman". Charming Helen, I'm sure.

I really fought for my freedom in that place (NHS Institution) and they were totally right not to give it to me. They learned their lesson the one time they did. My husband had a real go at them as I went straight into the nearest town, Haddington, and spent over £1000 on clothes. A friend of ours found me in the shop and reported me to my husband. It felt like he had spies everywhere!

I gave this friend some cards to post for me to friends. I didn't have any stamps and given that I only had a credit card, I felt I couldn't go in to a shop for a few stamps. She ended up giving the cards to my husband which I was most cross about at the time but having read them now that I'm well, I am very pleased they weren't posted. Let's just say I didn't come across very well in them!

I used to scour the building for escape routes through open windows and unlocked doors. I used to throw myself at doors hoping that I would fly through them like they do in the movies but it wasn't happening. I wasn't allowed to use my mobile phone either but used to sneak onto the balcony when the cleaners had left the door open as this was the only place I could get a reception and call my friends. By the time I got to make a call, I was so desperate to speak to someone that my friends must have thought from my calls that I was in the right place!

I was very crafty too even in my depressed state. In fact, I was probably even more crafty that I am normally actually. It's amazing that that skill didn't dwindle.

My enjoyment of spending and shopping has always been there. It turned into an obsession while I was ill. I hadn't been shopping for weeks since my blip in Haddington. It was far too long. It is probably the longest time I have ever been away from the shops. I was getting serious withdrawal symptoms.

I had had all my money confiscated in the hospital. In fact they search all of your bags that come in to the hospital and most things that make life bearable, like your phone and your purse, are taken away from you.

How do they expect you to get better without your 'survival kit'?!

I asked for a day out with my husband but then did a runner to Harvey Nichols, where I knew I could shop without my purse as I am a Personal Shopper customer and have my own account there. What could be better?

I took the train to Edinburgh. It proved to be a lot easier than I thought to get away with not buying a ticket (especially if you are as desperate as I was to get to Edinburgh. I would have done anything to get to Harvey Nichols that day!) as there were no barriers or guards policing the carriages.

I spent thousands of pounds on clothes and £600 alone on lingerie and was having a great time until I found myself being escorted out of the building by the security guards and taken back to the hospital. When my husband realised that I had gone missing, he knew immediately where I would be and he threatened (in a nice yet persuasive manner!) to get the police to come and pick me up. It was one of the only times that I remember having one of the so called 'manic highs' the doctors were always talking about but I soon came down to earth with a bump when the security guards turned up and my manic high funnily enough turned into an extreme low depression.

The security guards were very sympathetic but probably had little choice especially as I was giving them my sob story as I was been escorted out of the store. They still remember me. They always greet me when I visit the store and sometimes join me at the juice bar for a drink!

I've got over the embarrassment for the sake of my shopping you understand and didn't stay away for very long. It's a price I had to pay!

When I got back to the hospital, all the patients were lined up watching for my arrival. I didn't disappoint I have been told. I had to be dragged in kicking and screaming but made sure my Harvey Nichols bags came back with me.

My lingerie never made it to my room though.

I called the police station to file my report. "Yes madam, we'll be round to take your statement. What's your address?" Funnily enough, as soon as I mentioned Herdmanflat Hospital (NHS Institute), the line went dead. I was furious and called back with my "I am a law abiding citizen and pay my taxes. How dare you put the phone down on me"! I just reaffirmed that they had a mad woman on the line with such behaviour. I can see that now!

I must do a refresher on that book that my father gave me, "How to win friends and Influence People". I did a fantastic job of upsetting people during the worst days of my Depression.

Another psychiatrist who came to see me one evening while I was in the communal sitting room, looked like a student on the 'milk round' at university. I refused to see him very vocally saying that I wanted a doctor who hadn't just graduated and hadn't seen enough of life yet to even understand any of my issues.

What a brat!

I paid for that one though as one of the patients attacked me verbally accusing me of being a stuck up, arrogant bitch who had never had to work at anything in her life to get anything and did not know anything about the real world. Usually I am a complete wimp in such situations but the mood I was in I bit back with my life's story and we ended up being friends believe it or not. She was a lovely lady and I just seriously pissed her off! I am sure that my husband can relate to that too!

The trouble with depression is that it is not like my appendix had burst and needed to be removed. I wish it had. That's simple stuff. That's an operation, short recovery and ok, a physical scar but I'd rather that any day over the mental ones. I'm sure you'll agree with me on this one. Physical and mental scars heal, it's just that mental ones can take longer but you will get there.

I met quite a few lovely people in hospital actually. One guy was your typical 'Act first, think later' kind of guy who used to break peoples' legs for a living! He was always lovely to me though and told me that he would always look out for me, 'nudge nudge, wink wink'. Where on earth would I have met someone like that in my life? He's great. I think the world of him and he would do anything for me. I've used his name a few times to cheer up friends in difficult situations with my offer of last resort of sending round the 'heavies' to kneecap their perpetrators.

He even offered me his flat to live in (on my own! It was overlooking the sea too) when I told him that I wanted to leave my husband. I never felt threatened by him. Yet his outward appearance was very threatening. He had most of his teeth missing. He was covered in tattoos. He was always getting arrested for being drunk and disorderly. He loved his mum and dad though and would have done anything for them. I knew just from the way he talked about them that he wasn't a bad person. He'd just had some bad luck.

Another guy reminded me very much of Dell Boy out of 'Only Fools and Horses'. He was lovely too. He knew that I was new to Scotland and used to spend hours telling me local stories. He even made me a booklet of important numbers and addresses in Edinburgh. They were actually numbers that he considered to be important like drug pick-up points and shady second hand car dealerships. It's the thought that counts though.

We were forced to spend a lot of time together because there were too many of us and limited space. We used to spend all day in one of the two rooms and cry, stare at the walls or talk. The older people tended to sit in one room and the younger ones (under 60) used to stay in the other. No one bothered you if you wanted to sit on your own until duties. We all had to help out. We had to share kitchen duties and clearing up duties. We all had to take it in turns to set the tables at mealtimes and clear away.

I was in there for my Birthday and I remember my mother- and sisters-in-law bringing in cucumber sandwiches, scones and strawberries and cream. They even brought a table cloth and a rug. We were lucky to find a bench to sit on outside. The patients (or service users as they are now referred to) used to sleep on the benches during the day so there were rarely any free by visiting time. My sister-in-law said that it reminded her of a horror movie when the patients used to sit up in unison to get up to go in for dinner. In fact it disturbed her so much she told me that when they were leaving in the car she screamed "Floor it!" because she couldn't get out of the place quick enough. The whole place reminded me of a horror movie! It was very weird.

I was in one of the only two rooms on my own as I was considered to be a danger to myself and violent. I was only trying to escape. I wasn't planning to hurt anyone, unless they got in my way of course! Nothing, I came to the conclusion could be worse than that place.

Why had my husband left me there? He didn't love me. That had to be it. My mind was made up. My mind just went haywire.

I refused to see him or even speak to him. I hated him. I wanted a divorce. I never wanted anything to do with him. It was because of him that I was ill. He had alienated my friends and had shouted at most of them.

Now I know that it was to try and protect me from myself. Only he used to see what my nature of trying to be everything to everyone did to me. He reacted by trying to keep everyone away from me who he thought might put pressure on me. He did not know what else to do. He too felt isolated and alone.

He and my father were at loggerheads and no one has ever told me exactly what went on there. I can only imagine as they are both strong minded individuals who had their own ideas about the cause of and treatment for my illness; they blamed each other and they're both men of course so neither was willing to back down or apologise in the heat of the moment!

My sister was constantly battling to try and get them to see that pulling together with the common goal of getting me better and not fighting about who or what was to blame would be far more constructive. Alas the battle went on. My father was more forgiving but then he didn't have to put up with me 24/7 like my husband did.

After two more weeks the doctors and my husband agreed that I could go home but only if there would be someone there with me. The doctors, my husband and my father agreed that it would be best if my husband were to leave the family home and my father came up from Nottingham to look after me but you know what it's like. When you leave home, you don't want to go back to living with your parents. After two weeks we'd both had quite enough of that and we agreed he could go home to avoid the end of a beautiful relationship and more mental problems as a result of that and a whole new can of worms.

So unbeknown to my doctors and against all of their advice, I was left on my own and that's when I truly went off the rails.

LIBIDO, MY GOD IT'S BACK, GREAT! – HOW DO I STOP IT, IT'S RUINING MY LIFE?

Then overnight from being a depressed, withdrawn, anti-mojo 36 year old, overweight, humourless depressive, I became a slinky, sexy, funny, outgoing flirty cheap tart enjoying male company again. God, it was my 20s in London all over again but without the cash as I still wasn't earning.

It was like I had been in a coma. My drugs had been changed and reduced substantially. The drugs suppress everything, including your sex drive. I felt like I had woken up from a drugged induced sleep and was experiencing a reawakening in every way. Whatever it was, it was like my whole body and mind was waking from the dead. I felt alive for the first time in years.

The attention fed my ego and my self-esteem that had taken a real bashing over the past seven years and needed a lot of feeding. Please don't take my 'mojo' away again. I've got some making up to do.

I started dating men I would never have given a second look before. There was the multi pierced boy who I could have been his mother; the rugby player was a complete knob (he thought his knob was too big and "no rubber Johnny would fit it"!) with a shaven head who brought a tub of cheap ice cream in a plastic bag to the cinema. Then there was the doctor. He seemed like a safe bet until he too brought his own food to the cinema. This time it was a packed lunch! I had an epiphany with a religious nut who didn't think I was religious enough!

The antiques dealer, why I was with him I will never know. This was all about my libido and he was never interested! Still he thought that I should run away with him to America. I changed my mind and when I stalked him to say goodbye by hanging outside his house the morning of his departure, he called me a psycho. I questioned which one of us the most crazy given that he told me that he couldn't come to the door until he had showered and brushed his hair and teeth!

Another one bit the dust.

Several other unmentionable occasions followed and even in my manic state, alarm bells were ringing!

Was this another form of depression or a midlife crisis maybe? My doctor said that my diagnosis had changed from depressive disorder to bipolar depression and that my mania was probably 'Treatment-Emergent' which means that it was a consequence of all the treatment that I had received. He said that there are many variants of bipolar disorder and it is likely that I have a variant in which my mood only becomes high during times that I am taking antidepressant medication.

I felt like I was going through manic depression based on what I'd heard about it. I would have absolute HIGHS and then devastating lows. My psychiatrist recorded that my mood suddenly lifted and that I became elated, over-energetic and started spending excessive amounts of money. He was too polite to bring up my promiscuity.

I had no objections to highs in the beginning as it was the most fun I'd had in years. Not everyone agreed or believed me though. They said it was an excuse but it did coincide with my diagnosis being changed to bipolar depression! I begged my psychiatrist to stop it. He said that the treatment of a manic episode in someone who has had a lengthy depressive illness can be a delicate procedure and that I had had a lot of treatment in London before coming to East Lothian (including ECT, clinical psychology and many different antidepressants). When my mood suddenly became high a decision had to be made about using antimanic medication but there was a risk that this could cause my mood to plummet back into profound depression again so 'I was monitored'.

So I had to continue going through it and it seemed to go on for quite some time.

Personally I think it's worth going through this even if you risk getting into trouble as at least you feel alive. I just wish it had been with my husband but at this point I still thought that he hated me and I was still angry with him. It got me into lots of trouble.

After years of feeling numb and dead inside, I felt dangerously out of control and it was scaring me. One weekend I realised it had to stop. My special girlfriends from uni were having a girlie reunion in Bristol where we all studied - all those years ago. I hadn't joined them for a girlie get together since falling ill and decided this time to join them.

The weekend ran as most of our girlie weekends do: shopping, coffee and cake of course, take away dinner and out in the evening. I love girlie time, don't you? It all went wrong though during our evening out. We were all out in a nightclub having fun to begin with as we usually do. We were all getting chatted up but I took it too far when I kept throwing myself at one guy after another and I seemed to have forgotten who I came out with and who I was going home with.

My friends had had about as much as they could take and I don't blame them.

My friends dragged me out of the club and really gave me what for. "We've all come all this way (some of them from Europe and we only get together once a year because of children and other commitments we all have) and you spend all your time with strange men".

The reality of what I was doing hit home suddenly. I was distraught. I hadn't seen my best friends for five years and when I did I insulted them by treating them like this. When we got back to their house and I realised what I'd done, I just ran out of the house and fell to the ground crying my eyes out. How selfish was that? You do such out of character things when you're depressed. It's truly frightening. My friends have always come first in my life even above my husband. What was I doing? They've known me for 20 years and, thank goodness, know this is not how I would normally carry on.

One of the girls came to get me. One slapped me around the face. It was the only way to stop me crying hysterically. That certainly did the trick though. We went to bed after that and no more was said about it. God, what a weekend. I never want another one like that.

I'd also been spotted out in Edinburgh with various men and it had got back to my mother-in-law about my antics with the opposite sex. I was hurting people and it had to stop.

By this time six months had gone since I had been set free from my hospital life and my husband had left the family home and I realised that I really wanted my husband back after finally being able to rationalise his situation.

He'd had five years of trying to keep me alive for goodness sake. He needed help too. He had been terrified that I was lying again, that I would get out of hospital and try to kill myself again. Depressives are very good at lying, aren't we!

My husband knows that I went off the rails and knows that it was part of my Depression but how could I possibly expect him to come back? He'd have to be mad to come back, wouldn't he?

I went to my psychiatrist again and told him that my unacceptable antisocial behaviour was ruining my life and everyone else's. That's when he increased my dose of the antidepressant, Depakote. At the time I didn't realise that that was to try to control my highs.

I needed something. I even wanted to jump on him. Every man I saw I would imagine what it would be like to have sex with them. I often thought seriously about pulling guys over in cars over and asking for a quickie on the hard shoulder.

I was out of control; I could do nothing about it. Life was becoming impossible. I feel sorry for men if it really is like that for them the whole time and they think about sex every five seconds. I mean how can you get anything done?

I had even embarrassed myself with my life coach. I searched hard for a highly recommended one and found him in Cambridge. Not easy when you live in Scotland. He was lovely – gorgeous actually. He asked me what type of man I went for and what did I answer? "One like you really" and continued to list his attributes such as intelligent, slim, good looking. How embarrassing, that I actually threw myself at my life coach. The guy was trying to help me sort my life out. His questions moved on to orgasms with men. Given how attractive I found him I thought better of going back. He wouldn't have been safe. I could tell he was single because of the state of his cloakroom (as only a woman can!) but I cancelled my last appointment to avoid getting myself in to trouble.

The doctor was right. It did seem to be linked to medication as I'm not like that at all now.

My husband and I did try again but there was just too much resentment on his part and too much defensiveness on my part. After putting up with years of my Depression, being kicked out of his own home (as he used to put it) and the 'affairs' as he referred to them, too much water had passed under the bridge and we couldn't move forward from that. In hindsight, I wish that we had had some couple counselling but my head tells me that he is much better off without me and that we are better off as friends. I care so much for him that I just want what's best for him. I feel very lucky that we still have a very good relationship and I know that he is always there for me as I am for him. I don't know if I've actually told him that but I am! A very good friend of ours has said that we are both good people and were very good together but were dealt a bad deck of cards. Unfortunately that happens to a lot of good people but he has even said to me that maybe my illness was for the reason that I can now help others. That just shows you what kind of person he is!

I am ashamed of my behaviour but prefer to refer to my aberrations as just that. I did not see anyone until my husband and I were apart. Not that that is any excuse. In the past he talked about getting some therapy himself. I know that lots of carers feel that they need therapy. He's done so well since we split up. He hasn't got that pained look about him anymore. He has me to thank for that! I asked him recently if he wanted me to send him some more of the sleeping herb, Valerian, which he used to take to help him sleep. Apparently he doesn't have that problem any more. He has me to thank for that too! His film tracking and consulting business is now taking off again. Obviously that has been hard work given the jobs he cancelled, the work that he turned down and the leads he didn't follow up to look after me. Work used to take him away for long periods of time and it soon dries up if you don't take it when it's offered. However I hope to see him in the credits for a few things again soon!

Yes, I've been selfish but selfish in everyone's eyes but my own. I couldn't see that I was being selfish. I wasn't depressed on purpose or intentionally being selfish. Depression is a selfish illness. It makes the person who's ill selfish but certainly not because they want to be. I didn't want to feel this way. I didn't want to hurt anyone. It wasn't for attention and I didn't want anyone's help or time. I just wanted to be on my own.

I have such great family and friends. All my friends have always stood by me. They had faith that I'd pull through even though I certainly didn't have any faith in me. We all need someone to help us get through it. You'll know who it is for you.

LIFE JUST ISN'T FAIR

"Please shut up! I'll do anything,
I'll buy you a Porsche!"

To say that the last 10 years have been pretty grim would be an understatement. Most of my friends and family had not seen much of me during those years. It was probably better for everyone concerned as it happens! I'd either hidden myself away or been 'locked away' for a lot of that time. It seems pretty unbelievable that I've been depressed for almost a quarter of my life.

After my mum's death I appointed myself as the mother in the family. Whenever there were problems I felt I had to be the one to resolve them and then I became ill. Suddenly my family was having to look after me. You'd think that was sufficient for us to deal with but then life decided to throw more at us.

The first instance I have already mentioned is the first time when I nearly lost my sister to pancreatitis. It was so shocking and so sudden and as you can imagine my father now had two of his children to worry about and that's when the toll started to show on my father. Having got through the other side of my sister's first illness, then came the devastating news that she had cancer but let me paint the picture of why it was even worse than this originally sounds.

Having finally made the decision to have a child on her own after waiting for many years to find the right man like many of us had, my sister was diagnosed with breast cancer. She was seven months pregnant. This was the start of the many times my father had to cancel well needed trips. My sister had to have an emergency caesarean and begin her cancer treatment. She wasn't to have skin to skin contact with her son again for a year.

During this really difficult time I added to the family pressure as I was starting a week long major court case at the High Court in London that I had been working towards for over four years.

It was devastating to watch her going through losing her long beautiful hair and her unselfish acceptance at not being able to touch her son and her fear about not being able to see him grow up but being Liz, she got through it with laughter. Something I recommend for all of us.

She laughed as I gardened in my designer clothes (I wasn't expecting to be doing any of this. I hate gardening!) . She was bent over with laughter as she made me roll under the broken garage door in oil to get the gardening tools the day before she went in for her mastectomy. She smiled also at the garden as it looked amazing by the time we had finished. Wish I could say the same for my clothes.

After her operation I was determined to get her on to the right diet to speed up her recovery but as they say old habits die hard and she resisted my attempts to force her to drink my healthy home-made juices and broccoli and cauliflower fuelled diet. “It’s a bit late for that, give me chocolate, I need the feel-good factor instead!” she once told me. I know she used to pour the juices down the sink while I wasn’t watching! She’s a stubborn devil and we are seeing that trait already in her wee boy. My dad is standing back and watching in delight. It’s payback time!

Even now my Depression induced selfishness raised its ugly head. I couldn’t help thinking that God had been so unfair. I was the one who wanted to die, who thought she had nothing to live for and yet it is my beautiful younger sister who gets struck down with cancer. I had been praying to be terminally ill for years and God had to give this dreadful illness to my sister who was about to have the baby of her dreams.

I told my sister this and she was really upset at how selfish I was being by turning the situation around to me. I hadn’t meant it like that at all. I just couldn’t understand why she had to be ill. I wanted to take the illness away from her so that she could enjoy her baby. My illness was still not letting me think straight.

I wasn’t the best of nurses or surrogate mothers. I used bribery for discipline, promising Thomas a Porsche when he grew up if he’d stop crying (God knows where I was going to get the money from!). Added to that I gave my sister iron tablets instead of pain killers. The placebo effect didn't work very well this time. Liz always joked that it would be me that killed her and not the cancer! I believe I almost did once when her temperature was over 40 degrees and I was swamping her with blankets because all I could see was her shivering. When we got to the hospital she had a very bad infection and luckily for us she came through the right side of her 50/50 chance of survival and is still with us today.

We did laugh though at my dad and my brother, two big powerhouses, as they used to practically fall through the door of Lizzy's hospital room with little premature Thomas in their arms. The nappy bag was thrown over my brother's shoulder with the supplies of bottles and nappies (not that they would have known what to do with them!). Talk about 'Two men and a Baby!'

Learning how to sterilise the bottles was also a moment of hilarity. My dad's fiancée says that she has never seen such concentration in a man's face.

Again from a selfish point of view, I really did wonder how I was going to cope looking after her and Thomas as I was still not myself and still spending far too much time in bed depressed. But according to my sister I did wonders for her especially with the meals that I created for her that she referred to as a work of art which helped her get her appetite back.

I think that a lot of people have reality check when they experience the near death of someone close. We've all had a reality check with the last few years. It's surprising the number of people who have said to Liz, "God, your cancer has really made me re-evaluate my life and focus on what's important!" Liz's witty retort is, "Well I'm pleased for you. It's not done a lot for me I can tell you. I didn't need to re-evaluate mine. I already had my priorities right!"

Today Liz's wee boy is an angel (most of the time!). It's taken me this long to be able to call him an angel. We didn't get off to the best start with me having to help look after him while my sister was ill. He was cursed with four months of colic which didn't help the new aunty-nephew relationship!

I went through a stage of wondering if I should have a baby before it was too late but my father put me in my place by telling me that babies aren't bought from Harvey Nichols with a money back guarantee after 28 days if you are not 100% satisfied! I've certainly realised just what hard work it must be to have children and I take my hat off to all those women who just seem get on with it. God, did I moan about my nephew, Thomas. So much so that I used to call him Tomarse! My sister used to get very upset about that, obviously! Anyway, I'm pleased to say that we are all friends again and one big happy family.

CONCLUSION

I'm on the mend finally and in the land of the living again having finally stopped taking the Happy Pills after several years. I am finally getting my energy back. I want to do things, learn things, see things and reach old age. I am still not as self-motivated as I used to be but I am getting there.

That is why I found Nigel, my personal trainer. With his help and Weight Watchers, hypnotherapy and self-discipline and less food basically, it took me just over a year to shift the extra four stones that gathered during my Depression. That's down to Nigel being a very patient personal trainer and a good listener and I can certainly recommend him.

Please make your goal to get happy. I've missed almost 10 years of my life. That is not me feeling sorry for myself, it's a fact. I am still not where I want to be in my life but I know now where I want to be and am working towards it and enjoying the journey. We all deserve that and I wish it for you too.

Despite the most horrible seven years, I think that I am nicer (my friends tell me that I've always been nice although I never saw it myself) and a more understanding person for having been through what I have been through. I feel very lucky that I am still alive and healthy and have been given the chance to do something with my life. My only regret is that I dragged my husband and family and friends through all of this with me.

Some of my friends are still very upset about what they saw me go through but unfortunately they actually remember more of it than I do due to my ECT treatment. Maybe I should send them along for a session to erase all the nasty memories too! My husband could do with a mega session to erase all the bad memories from his memory bank. Unfortunately you don't have a choice which memories it erases.

It is generally a case of baby steps; literally, each little accomplishment deserves its own reward. Getting out of bed, eating breakfast, getting dressed - all baby steps. You need to give yourself time and treats. Aim for improvement, not perfection.

It is so true that every little helps, yet we so rarely give ourselves credit for the little things that we take for granted. I tried to congratulate myself for each little achievement. They took me one step closer to my ultimate goal of getting better.

Stop looking at your feet in despair. Begin to look up. It's amazing what you'll see that can make you smile. When I finally noticed that squirrel and didn't see it as grey vermin but cute and cuddly, I knew I was starting to see the light again! Appreciate every day as you live it. See a beautiful day as simply as it is. Achieving simple things leads to bigger successes and rewards. Little advancements make for quality of life.

Don't expect too much along the way and then everything becomes a bonus thereafter.

Praise yourself, lose the guilt and always remember you are only human. An individual with your own needs, qualities and special ways and quirks which more people than you realise will appreciate and love about you.

Start every day with something good, anything good about you. Say something positive to yourself in the mirror every morning, such as it's going to be a good day, well done you've got out of bed, or even that you have lovely blue eyes (unless of course they're still looking bloodshot!). Eventually, the list will get longer but be patient. One thing is bloody good and that's an achievement – it really is. The fact you have got out of bed to look in the mirror is another good achievement – remember baby steps!!!

Go to therapy, whatever works, even my cynical sister now goes to therapy and it is working for her. She goes to counselling and makes sure she has her feet massaged regularly. Her massage treatment for her brain and her body she calls it.

Treat yourself and go to a beauty therapist like your hairdresser once in a while - this works for men and women. Try acupuncture, reiki, hypnosis, counselling, crystals, candles, spas, relaxation classes, mediation, yoga, homeopathy .... Whatever makes YOU feel good.

Your will may be weak right now, but your imagination is more powerful than you know, use it to your advantage. Visualise how you want to be, keep it simple, see yourself up and dressed and ready to have breakfast or out having fun with friends again. Remember baby steps – don't imagine big impossible things, NOT that you are a film star going to your 1st Premier – that will come later if that is what your heart desires. Be realistic, set your goals so that you can achieve them and reward your goals.

SMILE as you take each baby step. A smile costs nothing yet creates so much more. It takes more energy and muscle power to frown than smile so why frown? A smile is not only free but actually can lift you and your spirits and is contagious.

From there you can laugh – remember that wonderful feeling when you laugh?

This book is not meant to be the answer to everything about depression. It couldn't possibly be, it's too big a topic. If you want more information go to the website, depressioncanbefun.com, the answers may be there. If not you can email me through the website or ask on one of the forums.

I hope I haven't offended anyone by writing what I feel and if I have affected anyone, I hope it is positively.

If you loved my book and found it helpful, I have achieved what I set out to do. If you hated my book and didn't get anything from it, you need another form of Therapy.

Good luck to you in your quest for happiness.

RELEVANT INTERNET SITES

Depression Can Be Fun
Email: info@depressioncanbefun.com
Website: www.depressioncanbefun.com

Filisa: Product ordering line: 01484 689 807
Email: enquiries@littleherbal-international.com
Website: www.littleherbal-international.com

Vegepa: Product ordering line: 0845 1300 424
Email: info@igennus.com
Website: www.igennus.com

FURTHER READING for you if you're the Depressive

Baker, Dr Dan and Stauth, Cameron (2004) What Happy People Know. St Martin's Press

Bloomfield, Dr Harold H. and McWilliams, Peter (1995) How To Heal Depression. Prelude Press

Brampton, Sally (2008) Shoot The Damn Dog: A Memoir of Depression. Bloomsbury

Burns, David D. (1999) Feeling Good – The New Mood Therapy. Collins Living

Cousins, Norman (2005) Anatomy of an Illness – as perceived by the Patient. Norton

Ellverton, Patrick (2004) Taming the Black Dog. Howtobooks

Gordon, James S. (2008) Unstuck. The Penguin Press

Griffin, Joe & Tyrrell, Ivan (2004) How To Lift Depression Fast. Human Givens Publishing

Harrold, Fiona (2001) Be Your Own Life Coach. Mobius

Holford, Patrick (2003) OPTIMUM NUTRITION for the MIND. Piatkus

Holford, Patrick (2007) FOOD IS BETTER MEDICINE THAN DRUGS. Piatkus

Jeffers, Susan (1988) Feel the Fear and Do It Anyway. Ballantine Books

Johnstone, Matthew (2007) I Had a Black Dog. Robinson Publishing

Klauser, Henriette Anne (2001) Write it Down, Make it Happen. Simon Schuster

Liebler, Nancy and Moss, Sandra (2009) Healing Depression the Mind-Body Way – creating happiness with meditation, yoga and ayurveda. John Wiley & Sons

Massey, Alexandra (2005) Beat Depression and Reclaim Your Life. Virgin Books

Peer, Marisa (2009) Ultimate Confidence: The Secret to Feeling Good About Yourself Each Day. Sphere

Plant, Jane and Stephenson, Janet (2008) Beating Stress, Anxiety and Depression: Groundbreaking Ways to Help You Feel Better. Piatkus

Puri, Basant K. and Boyd, Hilary (2005) The Natural Way to Beat Depression. The groundbreaking discovery of EPA to change your life. Hodder and Stoughton.

Servan-Schreiber, David (2004) Healing Without Freud or Prozac: Natural Approaches to Curing Stress, Anxiety and Depression Without Drugs and Psychoanalysis. Rodale International Ltd

FURTHER READING if you are the carer, friend, spouse

Baker, Barbara (2003) When Someone You Love has Depression. Sheldon Press

Carr, Caroline (2007) Living with the Black Dog: How to Cope when your Partner is Depressed. White Ladder Press

Golant, Mitch Ph. D and Golant, Susan K. (1998) What to Do When Someone You Love Is Depressed. Henry Holt

Johnstone, Matthew (2009) Living with a Black Dog. Robinson Publishing

Jordan, Mary (2006) The Essential Carer's Guide. Hammersmith Press

Sheffield, Anne (1999) How You Can Survive When They're Depressed. Random House

Quilliam, Susan (1998) What to do When You Really Want to Help but Don't Know How. Transformation Press

FURTHER HELP:

Alcoholics Anonymous England, Scotland and Wales, UK
24-hour helpline 0845 769 7555
www.aa-uk.org.uk
Great Britain
www.alcoholics-anonymous.org.uk

ANXIETY UK (FORMERLY NATIONAL PHOBICS SOCIETY)
Helpline for people suffering from anxiety, phobias, compulsive disorders, or panic attacks.
08444 775 774 (Mon-Fri, 9.30am- 5.30pm)

AWARE
Support for people affected by depression in Ireland and Northern Ireland.
72 Lower Leeson Street,
Dublin 2,
Republic of Ireland
(01) 890303302 (Every day, 10 am-10 pm, Thur-Sun until 1am)
Email: wecanhelp@aware.ie
www.aware.ie

THE ASSOCIATION OF POST-NATAL ILLNESS (APNI)
Information on post-natal depression, and puts mothers affected by post-natal depression in touch with others suffering or who have suffered from post-natal depression.
145 Dawes Rd,
Fulham,
London SW6 7EB

020 7386 0868 (Mon-Fri, 10am-2pm)
www.apni.org

THE BRITISH ASSOCIATION FOR COUNSELLING AND PSYCHOTHERAPY (BACP)
Information and advice on counselling including list of accredited counsellors in your local area.
1 Regent Place,
Rugby,
Warwickshire CV21 2PJ
0870 443 5252
www.bacp.co.uk

THE BRITISH ASSOCIATION FOR BEHAVIOURAL AND COGNITIVE PSYCOTHERAPIES
Provides a directory of registered therapists for £2 including postage.
PO Box 9,
Accrington,
BB5 2GD
www.psychotherapy.org.uk

CALM
Helpline for young men who are depressed or suicidal.
0800 58 58 58 (Sat-Tue, 5pm to midnight) (Calls are free from landlines)
www.thecalmzone.net

CARERS LINE
Helpline providing advice and information for carers on any issue.
0808 808 7777 (Wed & Thur, 10am-12pm, 2pm-4pm) (Calls are free from landlines and most

mobiles)
Email: adviceline@carersuk.org
www.carersuk.org/Contactus

CARERS DIRECT
Information, advice and support for
carers.
0808 802 0202 (Mon-Fri, 8am-9pm, Weekends, 11am-4pm) (Calls are free from UK landlines)
Email: CarersDirect@nhschoices.nhs.uk
www.nhs.uk/CarersDirect

Citizens Advice
www.citizensadvice.org.uk
Citizens Advice Scotland
www.cas.org.uk

Couple Counselling (see Relate)
Couple Counselling Scotland
www.couplecounselling.org

CRUSE Bereavement Care
Information and advice for
people who are bereaved.
Cruse House,
16 Sheen Road,
Richmond,
Surrey TW9 TUR
020 8940 4818 (Helpline and Information line, Mon-Fri, 9.30 am-5 pm)
www.crusebereavementcare.org.uk

DEPRESSION ALLIANCE
UK Charity offering help to
people suffering from depression and access to groups run by sufferers themselves.

Email: information@depressionalliance.org
Email: groups@depressionalliance.org

www.depressionalliance.org
DEPRESSION ALLIANCE SCOTLAND
0845 123 2320 or 0131 467 3050 (Mon-Fri, 11am-1pm, 2pm-4pm)
Email: info@dascot.org
www.dascot.org
DEPRESSION ALLIANCE CYMRU
Email: info@journeysonline.org.uk
www.journeysonline.org.uk

HEALTH INFORMATION SERVICE
Information on all health-related subjects
and information on where to get treatment.
0845 4647 (24 hours)
www.nhsdirect.nhs.uk

HOPELINE UK
Gives support, practical advice and
information to anyone concerned for a young person
they know to be at risk of harming themselves.
0800 068 41 41 (Mon-Fri, 10am-5pm, 7pm-10pm. Sat &Sun 2pm-5pm) (Calls are free from BT landlines)
www.papyrus-uk.org

THE HUMAN GIVENS
A new approach to psychology
for emotional health and clear thinking.
www.hgfoundation.com

MDF (Manic Depression Fellowship)
The Bipolar Organisation is a user led charity working to enable people affected by Manic Depression to take control of their lives.

160 Self Help Groups nationwide.
Steady Self Management System 4 day course for 18-25 year olds.
0845 6340 540
Email: mdf@mdf.org.uk
www.mdf.org.uk

MIND (National Association for Mental Health)
PO Box 277
Manchester
M60 3KN
MindInfoline: 0845 766 0163 (Mon-Fri, 9am-5pm) (Standard call charges apply)
Email: info@mind.org.uk
Mind Legal Advice Service: 0845 225 9393 (Mon-Fri, 9am-5pm) (Standard call charges apply)
Email: legal@mind.org.uk
www.mind.org.uk

National Self-Harm Network
Support for people who self harm as well as people it directly affects like family and friends.
NSHN
PO Box 7264
Nottingham
NG1 6WJ
0800 622 6000 (7pm - 11pm)
Email: info@nshn.co.uk
www.nshn.co.uk

NHS National Electronic Library for Mental Health
Useful information for patients and caregivers.
www.library.nhs.uk/mentalhealth/

NO PANIC
Worldwide support helpline for sufferers of

Panic Attacks, Phobias, Obsessive Compulsive Disorder, General Anxiety Disorder and Tranqiliser Withdrawal
0808 808 0545 (10am-10pm) (Freephone)
www.nopanic.org.uk

OCD UK
Charity site run by to support sufferers.
Support Groups
Email: **admin@ocduk.org**
www.ocduk.org

PACE
Counselling, mental health advocacy and group work for lesbians and gay men.
020 7700 1323
Email: info@pacehealth.org.uk
www.pacehealth.org.uk

PARENTLINEPLUS
Helpline and information for parents in distress.
0808 800 2222
www.parentlineplus.org.uk

RELATE
Offers face-to-face, phone or website relationship advice, counselling, therapy and mediation for couples or individuals.
03001001234
www.relate.org.uk

RETHINK
National Mental Health Charity working to help everyone affected by severe mental illness recover a better quality of life. Services include helplines; carer support;

community support; nursing and residential care and services dedicated to black and minority ethnic communities
Freephone helplines offering practical and emotional support and signposting to those experiencing severe mental illness, their carers and relatives.
General Helpline: 08454560455 (10am-2pm Mon – Fri)
Email: info@rethink.org
Email: advice@rethink.org
www.rethink.org

ROYAL COLLEGE OF PSYCHIATRISTS
Information about mental illness.
www.rcpsych.ac.uk

SEASONAL AFFECTIVE DISORDER ASSOCIATION (SADA)
Information and advice
PO Box 989,
Steyning,
BN44 3HG
England
www.sada.org.uk

THE SAMARITANS
Confidential emotional support to anyone who is suicidal or despairing.
Chris
PO Box 9090
Stirling
FK8 2SA
08457 90 90 90 (24 hours, every day)
ROI: (01)850 60 90 90
Email: jo@samaritans.org

SANELINE
0845 767 8000 (daily 6pm-11pm)
Email helpline: sanemail@sane.org.uk
Email: info@sane.org.uk

SCOTTISH ASSOCIATION FOR MENTAL HEALTH
Support, information and advice on various aspects of mental health.
Cumbrae House,
15 Carlton Court,
Glasgow G5 9JP
0800 917 3466
0141 568 7000
Email: enquiries@samh.org.uk
www.samh.org.uk

UKPPG (United Kingdom Psychiatric Pharmacy Group)
Information for people who use services, carers and professionals
www.ukppg.org.uk
www.choiceandmedication.org.uk

TURNING POINT
Social care organization providing a range of different services across England and Wales for people affected by mental health problems, drug and alcohol misuse.
Service Information: 02074817600
Email: Info@turningpoint.co.uk
www.turningpoint.co.uk

YOUNGMINDS PARENTS helpline
Helpline for parents on young peoples' mental health.
0808 802 5544 (Mon & Fri, 10am to 4pm, Wed 6pm to 8pm) (Calls free from

landlines and mobiles)
www.youngminds.org.uk

ALTERNATIVE FURTHER HELP:

British Acupuncture Council (BAcC)
63 Jeddo Road
London
W12 9HQ
020 8735 0400 (Mon-Fri, 9.30-5.30pm)
www.acupuncture.org.uk

The British Wheel of Yoga
01529 306851
www.bwy.org.uk

Institute of Complementary and Natural Medicine (ICNM)
Can-Mezzanine
32-36 Loman Street
London
SE1 0EH
020 7922 7980
Email: info@icnm.org.uk
www.i-c-m.co.uk

The General Hypnotherapy Register
PO Box 204
Lymington
SO41 6WP
www.general-hypnotherapy-register.com
Email: admin@general-hypnotherapy-register.com

The International Society of Professional Aromatherapists
www.the-ispa.org

Tai Chi UK Directory for the Healing Arts
020 7407 4775
http://www.taichi.uk.com

APPENDIX

1 Diagnostics for Depression

According to the Diagnostic and Statistical Manual of Mental Disorders that nearly every practising psychiatrist and psychologist uses, to summarise, the diagnostic criteria for an episode of major depression are: (This is obviously a bit technical as it is taken from the manual but it is nevertheless interesting)

At least five of the following symptoms have been present during the same two-week period and represent a change from previous functioning: at least one of the symptoms is either (1) depressed mood or (2) loss of interest or pleasure.

1. Depressed mood most of the day, nearly every day, as indicated by either subjective account or observation by others.
2. markedly diminished interest or pleasure in all, or almost all, activities most of the day, nearly every day (as indicated by either subjective account or observation by others of apathy most of the time)
3. significant weight loss or weight gain when not dieting (e.g. more than 5% of body weight in a month), or decrease in appetite nearly every day
4. insomnia or hypersomnia (sleeping too much) nearly every day
5. psychomotor agitation or retardation nearly every day (observable by others, not merely subjective feelings of restlessness or being slowed down)
6. fatigue or loss of energy nearly every day

7. feelings of worthlessness or excessive or inappropriate guilt (which may be delusional) nearly every day (not merely self-reproach or guilt about being sick)
8. diminished ability to think or concentrate, or indecisiveness, nearly every day (either by subjective account or as observed by others)
9. recurrent thoughts of death (not just fear of dying), recurrent suicidal ideation without a specific plan, or a suicide attempt or a specific plan for committing suicide.

In addition to these diagnostic criteria, many psychiatrists and psychologists recognise as additional diagnostic indicators the presence of generalised anxiety or panic attacks, phobia, paranoia, feelings of hopelessness and helplessness, irritability, anger and hostility, social withdrawal; and a range of physical changes or symptoms, including complaints of nausea, constipation, stomach cramps or pains, chest pains, rapid breathing, sweating, coldness, numbness or tingling of the feet or hands, headache, and feelings of pressure in the head, ears and neck. Sometimes, the depressed person with such physical symptoms may believe s/he has a terrible disease. To be diagnostically significant, the preceding psychological and physical symptoms must be seen as accompanying the persistent mood disturbance and loss of pleasure that define the core of depression, and can be ruled out as symptoms of another physical or mental illness other than depression.

2 The Right Diet Balance

Glucose is fuel for the brain, protein provides the building blocks of the happy chemicals in your brain called neurotransmitters (the chemicals that communicate mood) and fat makes up the majority of the brain itself (about 60%).

3 Types of Therapy

Psychology

Psychology is concerned with all aspects of behaviour and the thoughts, feelings and motivation underlying such behaviour. Psychologists have specific training in counselling and various forms of therapy and work with clients to help with problems like depression, relationship breakdowns and grief. Psychologists can teach clients many strategies to help them deal effectively with depression. They can also look at any underlying issues that may be causing or worsening the depression and work on these with clients and help them to develop more helpful ways of thinking and behaving that can make a significant difference. They are not medical doctors, and they tend to deal with more emotional issues than with clinical issues. For example, someone suffering from low self-esteem would visit a psychologist rather than a psychiatrist because they do not have anything physically wrong with them; they just need to talk things out. A person with schizophrenia would visit a psychiatrist because they would need medication to correct the chemical imbalance in their brain. Psychologists usually work with the backup of a GP to prescribe any medication that may be needed.

Psychiatry

Psychiatrists are medical doctors who have qualified in Psychiatry. While psychiatrists are medical doctors first, many have the same skills in counselling and talk therapy as psychologists. A psychiatrist is a physician who deals with mentally ill patients. Psychiatrists are medical doctors, so they can prescribe medication. As a result, they usually deal with clinical issues such as schizophrenia and manic depression whose treatments tend to require medication.

Psychotherapy
Individual, Group, Couple and Family Psychotherapy are all forms of psychotherapy. Psychotherapy helps people overcome stress, emotional problems, relationship problems or troublesome habits. A psychotherapist may be a psychiatrist, psychologist or other mental health professional who has had further specialist training in psychotherapy.
A psychotherapist may be a psychiatrist, psychologist or other mental health professional who has had further specialist training in psychotherapy.
A psychoanalyst usually deals with emotional issues and does not prescribe medication. Their approach is different from that of conventional psychologists. Psychoanalysis is a method of searching through a person's subconscious memories for the source of their current difficulties, rather than focusing on conscious memories. Psychoanalysts also tend to meet much more often with their clients. They usually prefer to meet as often as three to five times a week. Rather than the normal once a week that is common with psychologists.

4 Diagnoses

Depression strikes in several forms. When a psychiatrist makes a diagnosis of a patient's illness, he or she may use a number of terms:

- According to severity – mild, moderate, severe
- Reactive vs. Endogenous

- Bipolar Disorder
- Seasonal Affective Disorder (SAD)
- Dysthymic Disorder
- Cyclothymic Disorder
- Post Natal Depression (PND)
- Clinical Depression

To explain briefly what these mean (you don't have to read them all. Just skip to the one that is relevant to you):

- A medical practitioner judges the severity of the depression but generally mental experts say the key to judging this graduation is the change in someone's normal patterns and the loss of interest and a lack of pleasure in them. An Olympic swimmer, for instance, who began to fail to turn up for practice frequently, might be suffering from major depression. The more severe the depression, the more it is likely to affect its sufferer's life.

- Reactive Depression is a term used for depression thought to be caused by a specific event or circumstance, such as relationship problems or loss of someone you love either through death or the end of a relationship, losing or changing jobs or anything else you find traumatic. This does not refer to grief which is normal and healthy and temporary but to depression when it lasts well past the time that you would expect to start recovering from grief.

- Endogenous Depression is depression with no obvious cause – that was not brought on by a specific life event of circumstance, but rather appeared to come from nowhere.

Both are related to chemical changes in the brain – however they differ in terms of 'which came first' – i.e. 'did the depression come first, making life's problems seem far greater than they are, or did life's problems bring on the depression.'

. Bipolar depression tends to be associated with alternating depressive and manic moods separated by periods of 'normal' moods. The two extremes of bipolar can also rapidly change from day to day or even from hour to hour.

Mania can manifest itself in lots of ways. Some include increased energy and activity, being over-talkative, overfriendly, increased sexual energy and a decrease in the amount of sleep needed, excessive spending and in severe cases, hallucinations or delusions. That's me! Often the feeling of the elevation of this mania is in itself addictive and can make the patient reluctant to let go of the depression – whether at a subconscious or conscious level - and can be a barrier to that person getting better. I have to say that after having been there myself, I can really relate to that. It was much better than clinical depression! The only reason I realised that it had to stop was because I was hurting too many people and getting deeply into debt. I used to spend thousands of pounds on mad shopping sprees on clothes, antique furniture and original paintings. My husband used to dread me coming home with bags or worse still delivery vans or deliveries. In fact he probably used to dread me coming home full stop. I couldn't afford the mania! You feel unstoppable in a crazy way. You feel alive, you go mad and do silly things like 'blow lots of money' (that the average Joe Bloggs like me can ill afford! If you're a pop star, of course, it's a different story!) or go on sexual frenzies. It feels even more manic given the extreme low depression that precedes the high. The two opposing moods are literally poles apart. I can totally understand how the rich and famous become addicted to the mania and in a strange way don't want to be cured because they can totally afford the exuberance of MANIA.

. Seasonal Affective Disorder is a subtype of depression. It arises from some peoples' sensitivity to seasonal changes in the amount of available daylight. People sometimes react emotionally to changes in the amount of daylight available. For example, with less sunlight in the winter, some individuals become depressed, sad and irritable. They want to sleep a lot and eat constantly. When spring arrives and with more day light, their mood lifts, they feel better and start getting their energy back.

. Dsythymic Disorder – Some people suffer with recurrent or long lasting depression. These people almost always seem to have symptoms of a mild form of the illness. A major depressive episode can hit a dysthymic person too; causing double depression, a condition that demands careful treatment and close follow up.

. Cyclothymic Disorder is a persistent instability of mood, with several stages of mild depression and mild elation. This condition usually develops early in adult life and pursues a chronic course, although at times the mood may be normal and stable for months at a time. Because the mood swings are relatively mild and periods of mood elevation may be enjoyable, this type of depression frequently fails to come to medical attention. Stephen Fry by his own admission has been diagnosed with Cyclothymic Disorder or Bipolar 'Lite' as he said the

Americans refer to in the States. Only in the States could the word 'Lite' be tagged on to a mental disorder. I love them for that! They always try and see the good when we Brits can only see the bad. After all, they know what they are talking about when they talk about mental illness and stress and unhappiness given that many have their personal therapists whom they admit they see more often than they see their best buddies. Americans aren't afraid to talk about their therapists and I wish we were more like them. I think they have a healthier attitude towards mental health than we do as they understand the importance of maintaining mental as well as physical health.

. Post Natal Depression is thought to be a form of major depression. This is due to the similarity of symptoms in the two conditions. About 10% of new mothers develop PND. It is most common in women who have already experienced some form of depressive illness. Most women suffer from a down feeling the first few days after giving birth. However those with PND experience symptoms that are more prolonged, severe and disabling. If not treated, PND can last for months or years.

. When you hear the term Clinical Depression, it merely means that the depression is severe enough to require treatment. When a person is badly depressed during a single severe period, he or she can be said to have had an episode of clinical depression. More severe symptoms mark the period as an episode of major depression.

Lightning Source UK Ltd.
Milton Keynes UK
UKOW021434130212

187224UK00001B/20/P